Contents

How to use this book

Each page has a title telling you what it is about.

Instructions look like this. Always read these carefully before starting.

This shows you how to set out your work. The first question is done for you.

This shows that the activity is an **Explore**. Work with a friend.

Sometimes there is a **Hint** to help you.

This means you decide how to set out your work.

Ask your teacher if you need to do these.

Read these word problems very carefully. Decide how you will work out the answers.

Sometimes you need materials to help you.

Counters

Writing large numbers

Add the cheques to see how much you have won.

1
£7
£10 000
£600 000
£300
£7000

1. £ 6 | 7,3 0 7

2
£2
£200
£400 000
£9000
£20 000

3
£300
£3
£60
£700 000
£8000

4
£900 000
£1
£900
£70
£80 000

5
£8
£400
£70 000
£30

6
£10 000
£9000
£40
£8
£300 000

7
£7000
£800
£500 000
£9
£90

8
£200 000
£90 000
£600
£20
£5000

9
£200 000
£500
£1 000 000
£6
£30 000
£4000

10
£9
£90 000
£900 000
£90
£900

e Write the amounts in order from smallest to largest.

Write the value of the 9 in each number.

11 94 618

11. 9 0,0 0 0

12 417 923

13 394 612

14 9117

15 1 904 721

16 309 002

17 581 729

Writing large numbers

Write each number in figures.

1 Sixty-eight thousand, seven hundred and fourteen.

1. 6 8,7 1 4

2 One hundred and forty-two thousand, and fifty-one.

3 Seven hundred and four thousand, six hundred and nine.

4 Six hundred and sixty thousand, two hundred and eleven.

5 Eight hundred and twelve thousand, and ninety.

6 Ninety-nine thousand and fifteen.

7 Three hundred and thirty-three thousand.

8 Two hundred and seventeen thousand, six hundred and six.

9 Four hundred and four thousand, five hundred and forty.

10 Sixty-five thousand and six.

Write the value of the 1 in each number.

11 718 294

II. 1 0,0 0 0

12 641 873

13 36 412

14 201 678

15 5491

16 500 160

17 1 046 293

4

Comparing large numbers

Place-value N1

> Write the correct sign between each pair of numbers.

1   704 218  940 218

I. 7 0 4 , 2 1 8 < 9 4 0 , 2 1 8

2   318 624  318 264

3   497 209  497 202

> Remember the crocodile eats the larger number.

4   250 681  205 681

5   500 239  500 299

6   720 340  702 430

7   891 998  819 998

8   901 999  902 000

9   543 345 534 554

10 602 694  598 992

€ Write I more than the larger number in each pair.

11 Sam had ticket number **476 204**.

 His friend had the ticket before. What number was it?

His mum had the ticket with a number **10** more than Sam's. What number was it?

Problems

12 Miss Moneypots sold her house for **£179 250**.

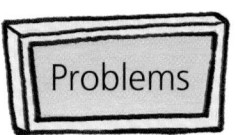 Mrs Diamond sold her house for **£197 650**. Whose house was worth more?

How much could Mr Big sell his house for, to get an amount between the two?

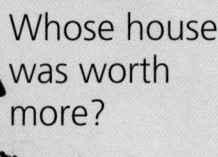

Ordering large numbers

> Write the distances in light years to the planets in order, from smallest to largest.

1
668 138 
875 981
756 343
857 909

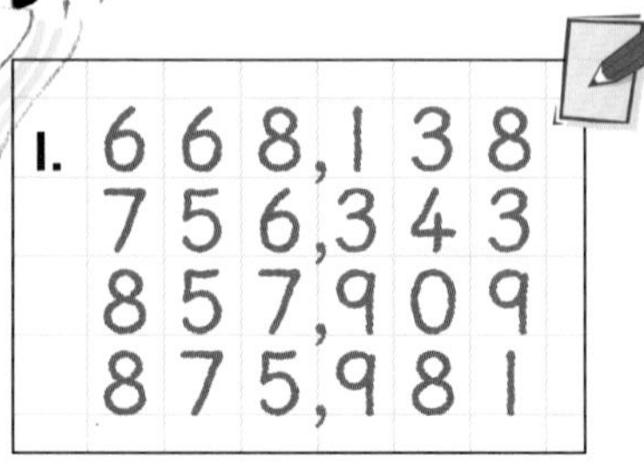

1. 6 6 8 , 1 3 8
   7 5 6 , 3 4 3
   8 5 7 , 9 0 9
   8 7 5 , 9 8 1

2
674 231   670 321 
647 231
607 231

3
990 741   909 742 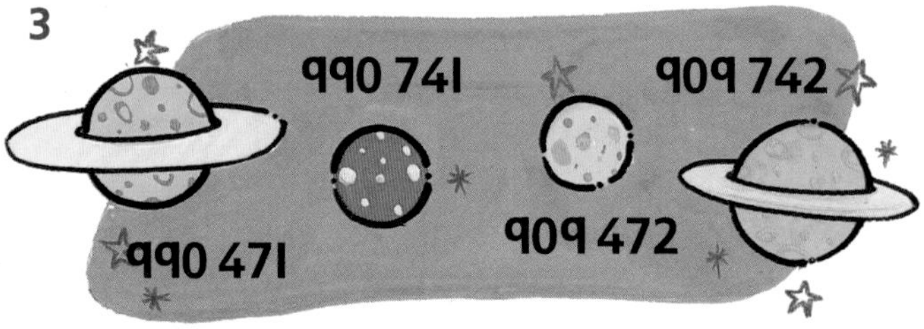
990 471
909 472

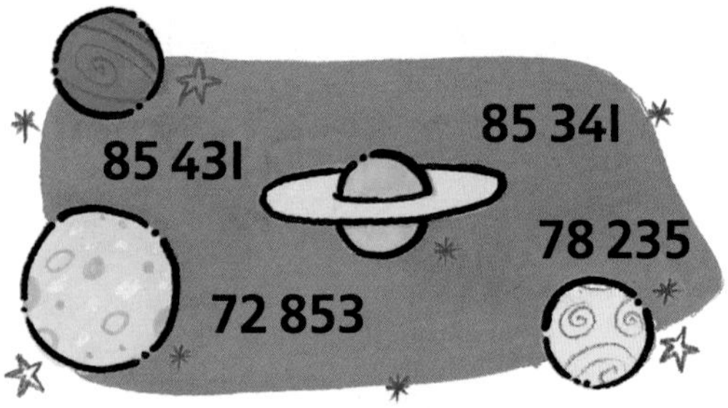

4
85 431   85 341
78 235
72 853

5
278 316 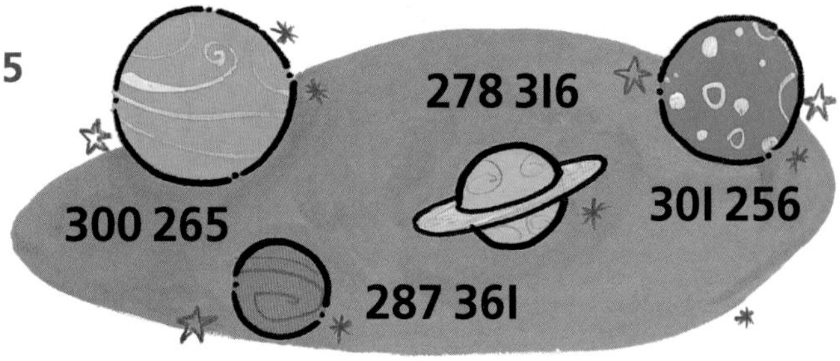
300 265
287 361
301 256

6
421 791 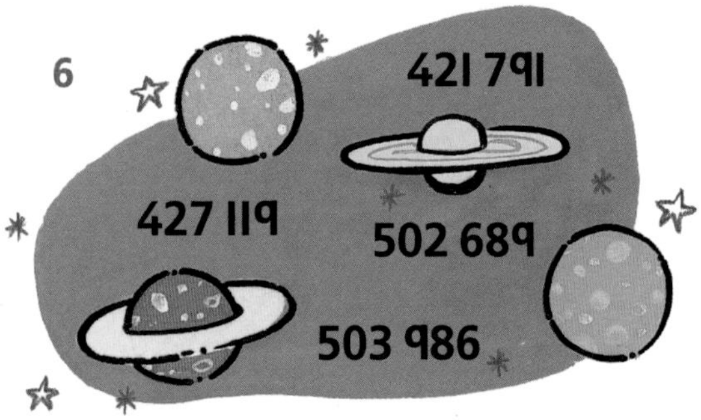
427 119   502 689
503 986

7
70 991 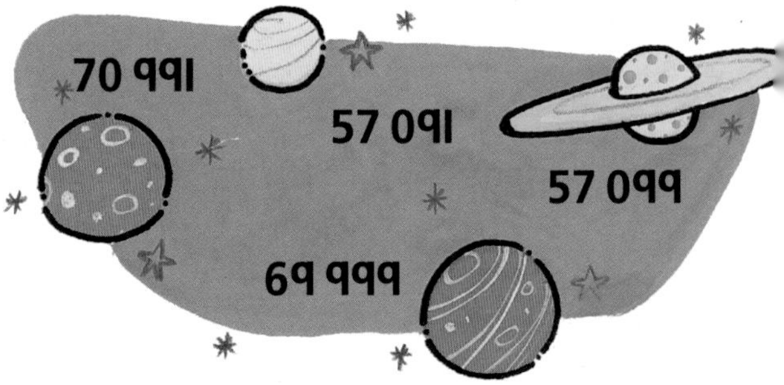
57 091
57 099
69 999

ℓ Which is the largest number? Which is the smallest?

Explore

Write the last 6 digits of your phone number.

Make the largest number you can using these digits.

Make the smallest.

Make the number nearest to 100 000,

200 000, 300 000, … 1 000 000.

My phone number: 357...
Largest number: 9753...

Rounding to the nearest 10

How far has each aeroplane flown to the nearest 10 km?

1. 1 4 7 2 km → 1 4 7 0 km

1472 km

2091 km

4207 km

1008 km

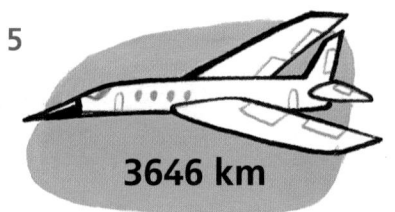

3646 km

2402 km

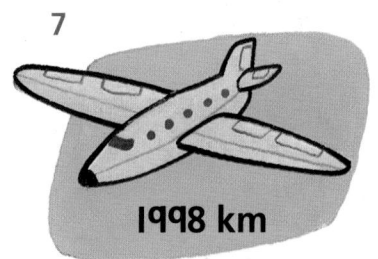

1998 km

8043 km

7951 km

9099 km

e Write how far each aeroplane has flown to the nearest 100 km.

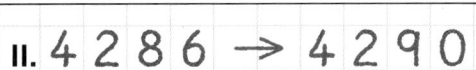

Round each number to its nearest 10.

11   4286

II. 4 2 8 6 → 4 2 9 0

12   2492

13   1059

14   6408

15   7264

16   9468

17   1047

18   6995

19   3051

20   9999

7

Rounding to the nearest 100

How many people were in each crowd to the nearest 100?

1  6750

1. 6 7 5 0 → 6 8 0 0

2 7549

3  6666

4 5452

5 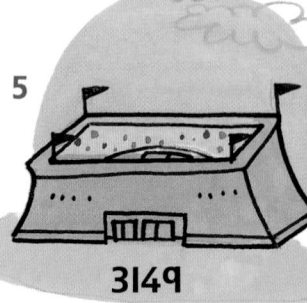 3149

6  2449

7 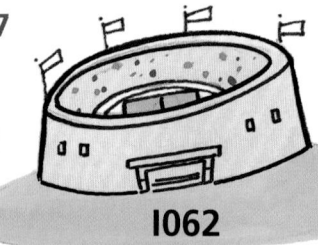 1062

8  1112

q  3451

10 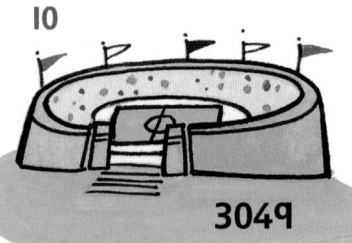 3049

11 7126

12  9294

13  8409

Round each number to its nearest 10 and its nearest 100.

14  1747

14. 1 7 4 7 → 1 7 5 0
    1 7 4 7 → 1 7 0 0

15  6104

16  7208

17 8792

18 2548

19 5498

20 3996

8

How much has each goalkeeper saved to the nearest £1000?

1. £7460 → £7000

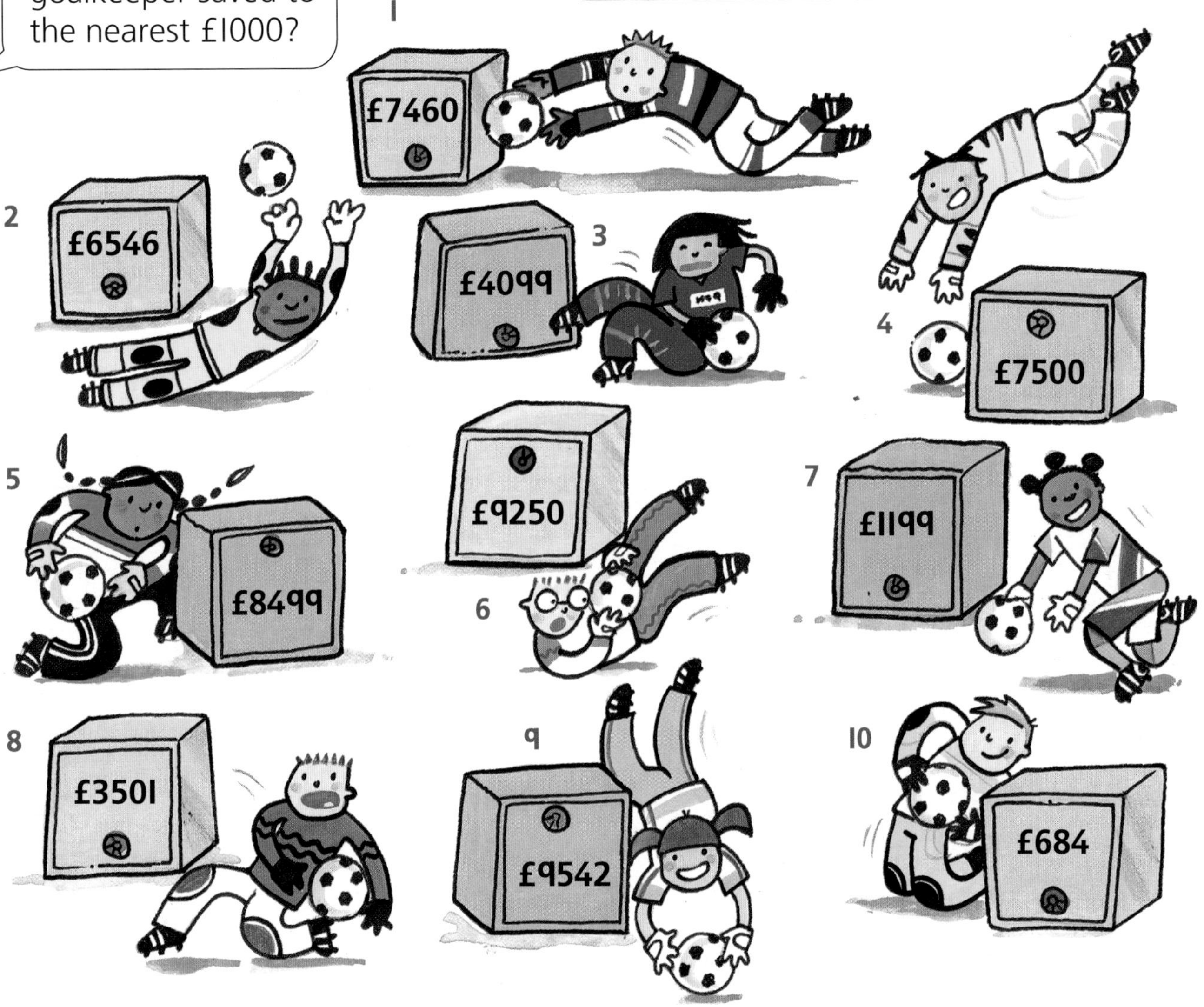

1 £7460

2 £6546

3 £4099

4 £7500

5 £8499

£9250

6

7 £1199

8 £3501

9 £9542

10 £684

℮ Write how much each player needs to save to have £10 000.

Explore

How many numbers less than 10 000 can you write where the nearest 10 is the same as the nearest 100 and the nearest 1000?

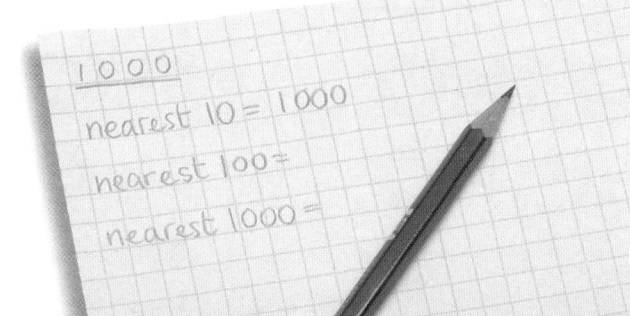

1000

nearest 10 = 1000

nearest 100 =

nearest 1000 =

Dividing

Write two divisions for each number. Use the grid to help you.

1. $15 \div 3 = 5, 15 \div 5 = 3$

1  2  3

4  5  6

7  8  9

10  11  12

13  14   15

1	2	3	4	5	6	7	8	9	10
2	4	6	8	10	12	14	16	18	20
3	6	9	12	15	18	21	24	27	30
4	8	12	16	20	24	28	32	36	40
5	10	15	20	25	30	35	40	45	50
6	12	18	24	30	36	42	48	54	60
7	14	21	28	35	42	49	56	63	70
8	16	24	32	40	48	56	64	72	80
9	18	27	36	45	54	63	72	81	90
10	20	30	40	50	60	70	80	90	100

Copy and complete.

16   $24 \div 6 = $ ◯

16. $24 \div 6 = 4$

17   $21 \div 7 = $ ◯

18   $18 \div 9 = $ ◯

19   $30 \div $ ◯ $= 5$

20   $30 \div 3 = $ ◯

21   $18 \div 6 = $ ◯

22   $56 \div $ ◯ $= 7$

23   $45 \div 5 = $ ◯

24   $28 \div $ ◯ $= 7$

25   $20 \div $ ◯ $= 4$

26   $64 \div 8 = $ ◯

27   $42 \div $ ◯ $= 7$

28   $48 \div 6 = $ ◯

Multiplying

Write the position of each cat.

1. $a = 14$

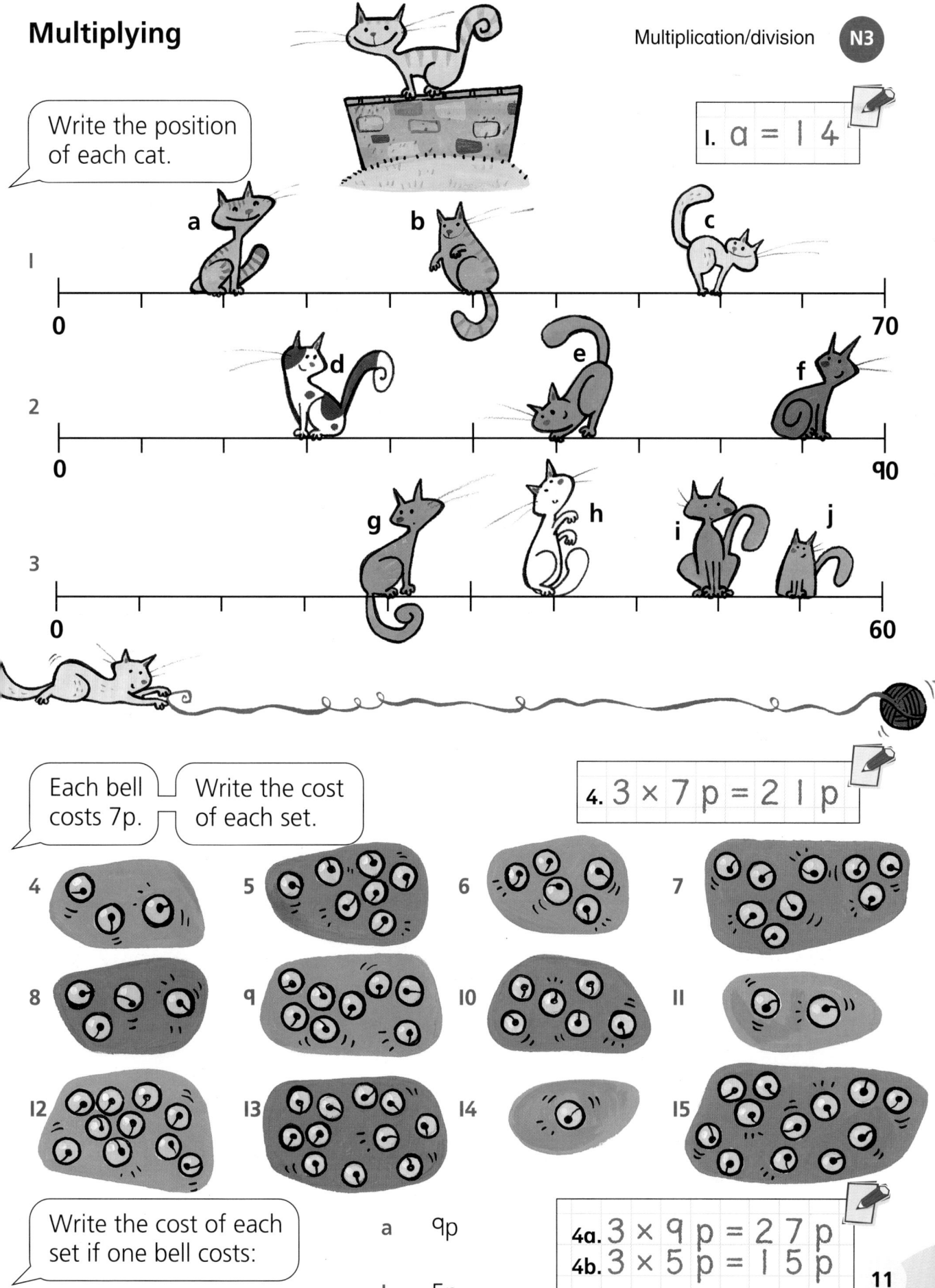

Each bell costs 7p. Write the cost of each set.

4. $3 \times 7p = 21p$

Write the cost of each set if one bell costs:

a   9p

b   5p

4a. $3 \times 9p = 27p$
4b. $3 \times 5p = 15p$

11

Multiplying and dividing

Copy and complete.

1 $3 \times$ 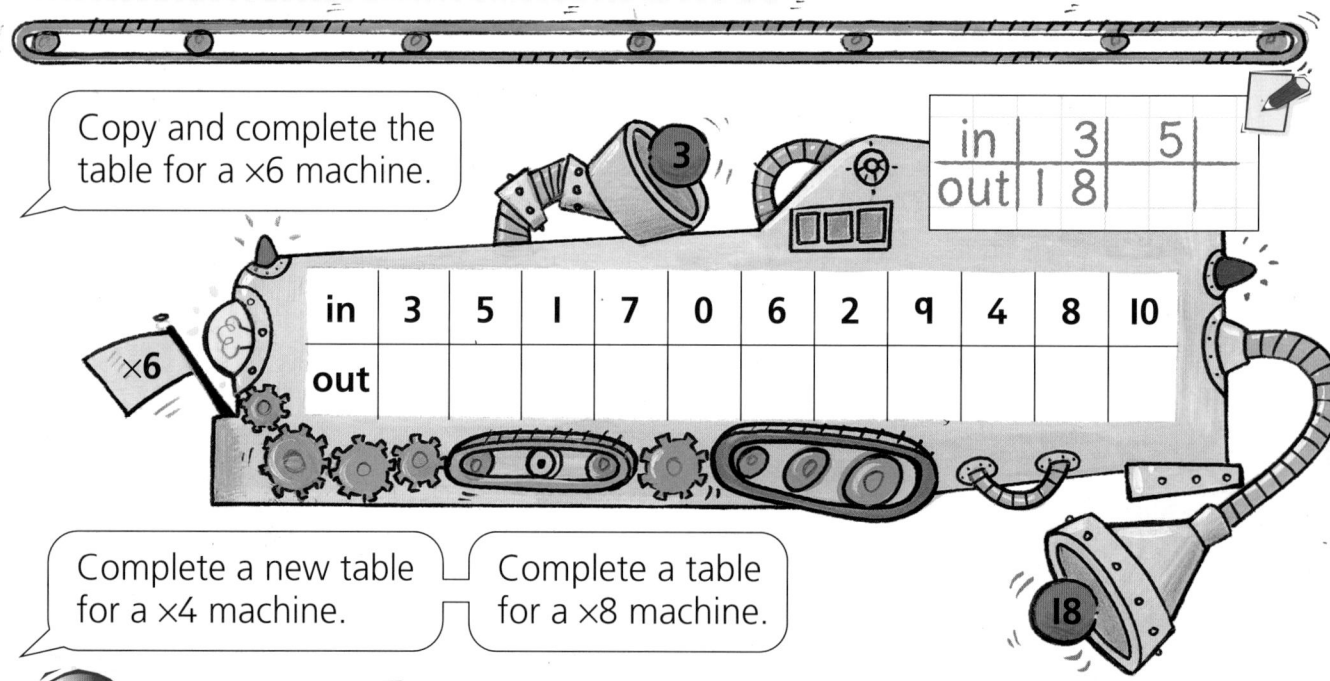 $= 15$

1. $3 \times 5 = 15$

2 $4 \times$ = 28

3 $20 \div$ = 5

4 $7 \times$ = 42

5 $24 \div$ = 3

6 $\times 9 = 45$

7 $21 \div$ = 7

8 $10 \times$ = 50

9 $54 \div$ = 6

10 $\div 5 = 8$

11 $7 \times$ = 56

12 $\times 9 = 36$

13 $\div 4 = 6$

14 $8 \times$ = 48

15 $36 \div$ = 6

16 $\times 4 = 16$

e Write a matching multiplication or division for each.

Copy and complete the table for a ×6 machine.

in	3	5	
out	1 8		

in	3	5	1	7	0	6	2	9	4	8	10
×6 out											

Complete a new table for a ×4 machine.

Complete a table for a ×8 machine.

Explore

Use number cards 4, 5, 6, 7, 8, 9.

Choose any two and multiply the numbers together.

How many different odd answers are possible?

How many different even answers are possible?

8 4

$4 \times 8 = 32$

Remainders

Four tyres are put on each car.	How many tyres are left over?

1. $18 \div 4 = 4 \text{ r } 2$
    2 tyres left

1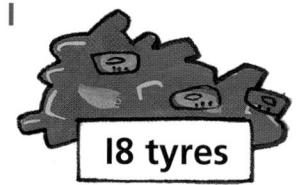
18 tyres

2
21 tyres

3
29 tyres

4
34 tyres

5
22 tyres

6
28 tyres

7
38 tyres

8
42 tyres

9
9 tyres

10
15 tyres

11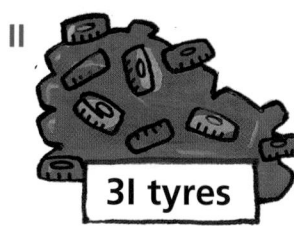
31 tyres

12
49 tyres

How many cars could have new tyres altogether?

0	40	80

Copy and complete.

13   $20 \div 8 =$

14   $44 \div 8 =$

15   $30 \div 8 =$

16   $76 \div 8 =$

17   $28 \div 8 =$

18   $4 \div 8 =$

19   $58 \div 8 =$

20   $54 \div 8 =$

13. $20 \div 8 = 2 \frac{4}{8}$
     $= 2 \frac{1}{2}$

Divide each number by 4.

13

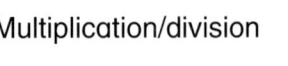

0   35   70

Complete these.

1    $54 \div 7 =$

1. $54 \div 7 = 7\frac{5}{7}$

2   $71 \div 7 =$ 3 $26 \div 7 =$ 4 $36 \div 7 =$

5   $32 \div 7 =$ 6 $16 \div 7 =$ 7 $59 \div 7 =$ 8 $43 \div 7 =$

9   $48 \div 7 =$ 10 $67 \div 7 =$ 11 $51 \div 7 =$ 12 $79 \div 7 =$

Eight pencils fit in a pack.

How many packs can be made with each set of pencils?

13. $22 \div 8 = 2\frac{6}{8}$
$= 2\frac{3}{4}$

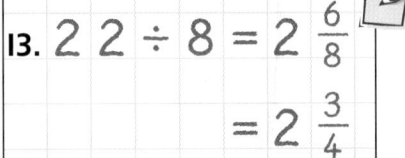

13 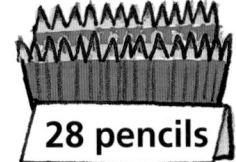 22 pencils   14 28 pencils   15 54 pencils   16 66 pencils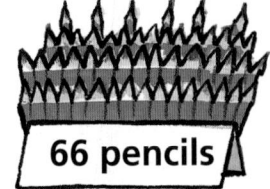

17 10 pencils   18 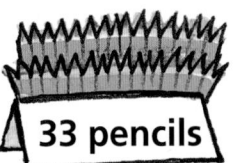 33 pencils   19 45 pencils   20 73 pencils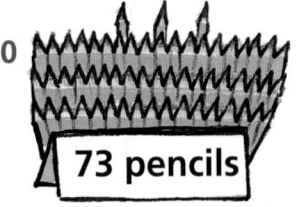

21 59 pencils   22 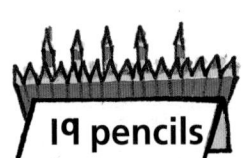 19 pencils   23 30 pencils   24 84 pencils

e How many packs can be made altogether?

Copy and complete.

1   42 ÷ 5 =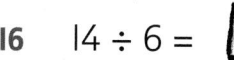

I. $42 \div 5 = 8\frac{2}{5}$

2   23 ÷ 4 =   3   50 ÷ 6 =   4   50 ÷ 7 =

5   27 ÷ 8 =   6   54 ÷ 5 =   7   69 ÷ 9 =

8   76 ÷ 7 =   9   42 ÷ 8 =   10   38 ÷ 6 =

11   80 ÷ 9 =   12   30 ÷ 7 =   13   30 ÷ 8 =

14   44 ÷ 6 =   15   50 ÷ 8 =   16   14 ÷ 6 =

Stamps are sold in books of 10.

How many books are needed?

17. $23 \div 10 = 2\frac{3}{10} = 2.3$
3 books needed

17
23 stamps

18
47 stamps

19
53 stamps

20
62 stamps

21
18 stamps

22
39 stamps

23
8 stamps

24
75 stamps

25
90 stamps

Explore

You have 61 fish.

How many fish does each penguin get if you divide them equally between 2 penguins, 3 penguins, 4 penguins, …?

$61 \div 2 = 30\frac{1}{2}$
$61 \div 3 =$

> The sock shop has a delivery of socks. ┤ Write how many socks.

I. double 4 6
80 + 12 = 92

1
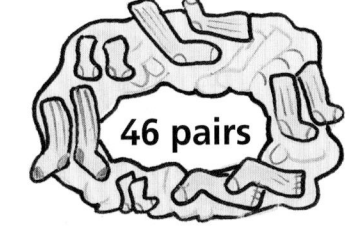
46 pairs

2
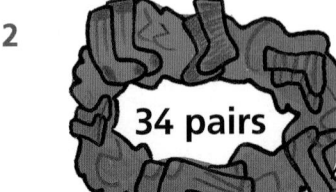
34 pairs

3
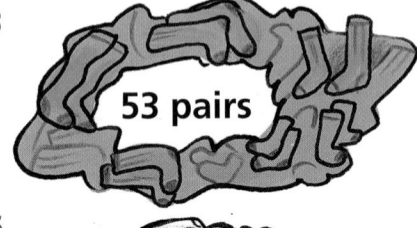
53 pairs

4
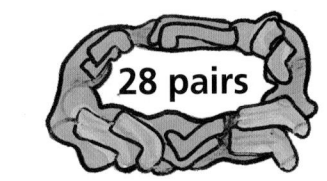
28 pairs

5
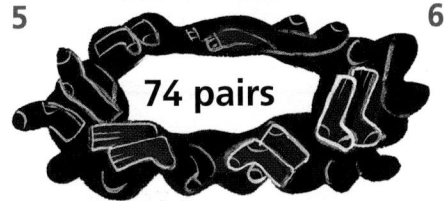
74 pairs

6
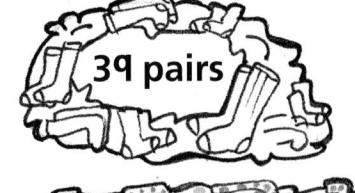
39 pairs

7
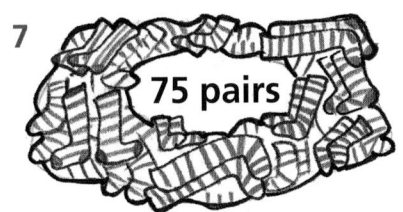
75 pairs

8

66 pairs

9
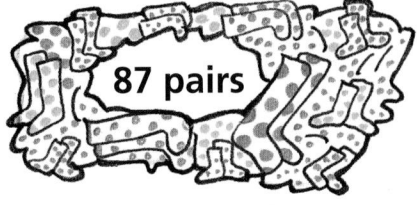
87 pairs

🅮 Each box can hold 12 pairs of socks. How many boxes are needed for each delivery?

> The socks in these boxes are sorted into pairs. ┤ Write how many pairs.

10. half of 6 4
30 + 2 = 32

10

64

11

86

12

48

13

124

14

166

15

96

16

78

17

154

18

136

Doubling and halving

Double each distance to find how far each journey is there and back.

1

320 km

1. double 3 2 0
600 + 40 = 640 km

2

240 km

3

460 km

4

170 km

5

580 km

6

650 km

7

280 km

8

790 km

9

830 km

10
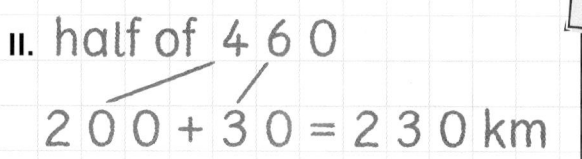
950 km

⊘ Halve each distance.

The distances are for return trips.

Halve each distance to find how far for a one-way trip.

II. half of 4 6 0
200 + 30 = 230 km

11

460 km

12

280 km

13

840 km

14

630 km

15

340 km

16

780 km

17

1270 km

18

1750 km

19

1150 km

⊘ Double each distance.

Doubling and halving

Write the cost of a pair of tickets.

1. double £ 4·3 0
   £ 8 + 6 0 p = £ 8·6 0

1 £4·30

2 £8·40

3 £3·15

4 £2·90

5 £3·60

6 £1·70

7 £1·80

8 £4·60

9 £2·50

e Write the cost of four tickets.

Tickets are half-price for children.

Write the cost of a child's ticket.

10. half of £ 4·2 0
    £ 2 + 1 0 p = £ 2·1 0

10 £4·20

11 £3·60

12 £5·40

13 £9·30

14 £8·70

15 £12·60

e Write the cost for one adult and one child.

Explore

Start with 30 and keep doubling.

How far can you go?

Try starting with other multiples of 10 (20, 50, …).

30 →   60 →   120 →

Multiplying and dividing

Copy and complete.

Write two matching divisions.

1   $3 \times 14 =$

2   $2 \times 17 =$

I. $3 \times 14 = 42$
$42 \div 3 = 14$
$42 \div 14 = 3$

3   $5 \times 18 =$    4 $16 \times 9 =$

5   $7 \times 15 =$ 6 $13 \times 11 =$ 7 $5 \times 17 =$

8   $14 \times 20 =$ 9 $8 \times 16 =$ 10 $9 \times 18 =$

🐛 Write another matching multiplication for each.

Write a multiplication for each set.

Write a matching division.

II. $£3 \cdot 20 \times 4 = £12 \cdot 80$
$£12 \cdot 80 \div 4 = £3 \cdot 20$

11
£3·20 each

12
£5·30 each

13
£10·90 each

14
£7·20 each

15
£1·10 each

16
£2·40 each

17
£1·30 each

18
£3·05 each

19
£6·10 each

19

Use the matching facts to write the missing numbers.

1. $8 \times 24 = 192$
    $192 \div 8 = $

1. $192 \div 8 = 24$

2. $9 \times 17 = 153$
    $153 \div 9 = $

3. $6 \times 33 = 198$
    $198 \div 6 = $

4. $5 \times 29 = 145$
    $145 \div 5 = $

5. $\_ \times 14 = 98$
    $98 \div 7 = $

6. $\_ \times 48 = 144$
    $144 \div 3 = $

7. $\_ \times 34 = 170$
    $170 \div 5 = $

8. $\_ \times 13 = 156$
    $156 \div 12 = $

9. $\_ \times 19 = 152$
    $152 \div 8 = $

10. $\_ \times 27 = 243$
    $243 \div 9 = $

ℯ Write two more facts for each.

Problems

$14 \times 11 = 154$

$8 \times 24 = 192$

$7 \times 35 = 245$

$19 \times 17 = 323$

$21 \times 13 = 273$

11. What is **14** multiplied by **11**?

12. What is **245** divided by **35**?

13. What is **192** divided by **8**?

14. How many lots of **8** in **192**?

15. What is $\frac{1}{7}$ of **245**?

16. What are **7** lots of **35**?

17. What's **13** times **21**?

18. How many sets of **14** in **154**?

19. What is $\frac{1}{8}$ of **192**?

20. How many **17s** in **323**?

21. What is **273** divided by **13**?

Multiplying and dividing

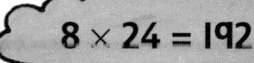

$8 \times 24 = 192$

$5 \times 35 = 175$

$7 \times 13 = 91$

$6 \times 48 = 288$

$3 \times 97 = 291$

Problems

1 Chocolate bars come in boxes of **6**.

How many boxes are needed for **288** bars?

2 Alex plays her guitar every day.

She started practising **91** days ago.

For how many weeks has she been playing the guitar?

3 Davinder is helping in the library.

There are **192** books and **8** shelves.

How many books should he put on each shelf so they all hold the same number of books?

4 Kara videos **3** episodes of her favourite programme.

She uses **291** minutes of video tape.

How long is each episode?

5 There are **24** children in the class.

They share a packet of crisps. If there are **192** crisps in the packet, how many does each child get?

6 Grandpa has **5** grandchildren.

He spends **£175** on Christmas presents for them.

How much does each grandchild's present cost?

Explore

Multiply some other numbers by 11, e.g. 23, 42, …

What do you notice?

$24 \times 11 = 264$

$41 \times 11 = 451$

Which of these numbers do you think divide by 11?

Look at the pattern of the digits.

144   297   781   683   594   891

How do you know? Does 858 divide by 11?

Write some other numbers that divide by 11.

Write how many pieces.

1 $1\frac{1}{4}$

I. $1\frac{1}{4} = 5$ quarters

2  $3\frac{2}{5}$

3  $4\frac{5}{8}$

quarters
thirds
halves
fifths
sixths
eighths

4  $3\frac{2}{3}$

5 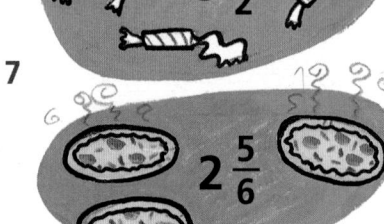 $5\frac{1}{2}$

6  $6\frac{3}{8}$

7  $2\frac{5}{6}$

8 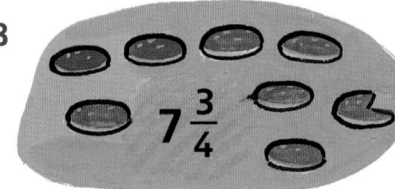 $7\frac{3}{4}$

9 $4\frac{4}{5}$

10  $6\frac{3}{10}$

11 $4\frac{7}{8}$

Write each amount as a fraction.

Ia. $1\frac{1}{4} = \frac{5}{4}$

How many twelfths?

12  $2\frac{7}{12}$

13  $1\frac{11}{12}$

12. $2\frac{7}{12} = \frac{31}{12}$

14 $3\frac{5}{12}$

15  $2\frac{1}{12}$

16 $5\frac{3}{12}$

17  $2\frac{9}{12}$

e Write the mixed numbers in order from smallest to largest.

Proper and improper fractions

Write the number of kilograms.

1

$\frac{1}{4}$ kg each

I. $\frac{7}{4} = 1\frac{3}{4}$ kg

2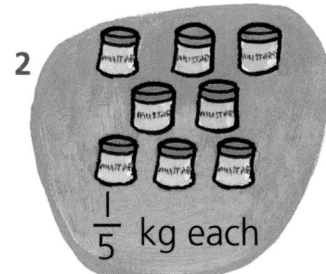

$\frac{1}{5}$ kg each

3

$\frac{1}{6}$ kg each

4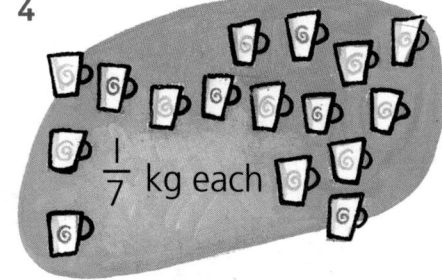

$\frac{1}{7}$ kg each

5

$\frac{1}{4}$ kg each

6

$\frac{1}{5}$ kg each

7

$\frac{1}{3}$ kg each

8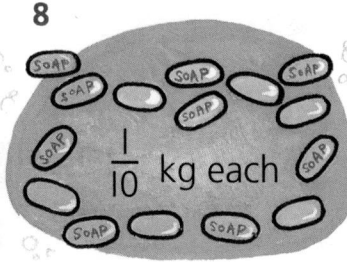

$\frac{1}{10}$ kg each

9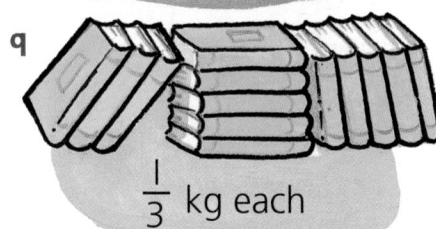

$\frac{1}{3}$ kg each

10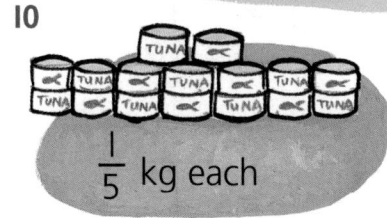

$\frac{1}{5}$ kg each

℮ Write the denominator for each fraction.

Write the fraction.

11
denominator 3
numerator 2

II. $\frac{2}{3}$
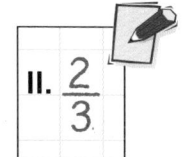

12
numerator 4
denominator 5

13
denominator 7
numerator 6

14
denominator 9
numerator 5

15
numerator 3
denominator 4

16
numerator 9
denominator 10

17
denominator 2
numerator 1

Fractions

> Write the number of hours.

1  6 nights of homework $\frac{1}{4}$ hour each

1. $\frac{6}{4} = 1\frac{2}{4} = 1\frac{1}{2}$ hours

2  7 stories $\frac{1}{3}$ hour each

3 24 songs $\frac{1}{10}$ hour each

4  7 games $\frac{1}{2}$ hour each

5 7 nights of homework $\frac{1}{5}$ hour each

6 13 stories $\frac{1}{6}$ hour each

7 20 songs $\frac{1}{8}$ hour each

8 $\frac{1}{3}$ hour each

8 programmes

9 18 times cleaning teeth $\frac{1}{12}$ hour each

10 17 games $\frac{1}{5}$ hour each

Problems

11 Write a fraction more than $\frac{1}{2}$, with a denominator of **4**.

12 Write a fraction with a numerator of **3** that is less than $\frac{1}{2}$.

13 Write a fraction with a numerator of **2** that is equal to $\frac{1}{4}$.

14 Write a fraction more than $\frac{2}{3}$, with a denominator of **6**.

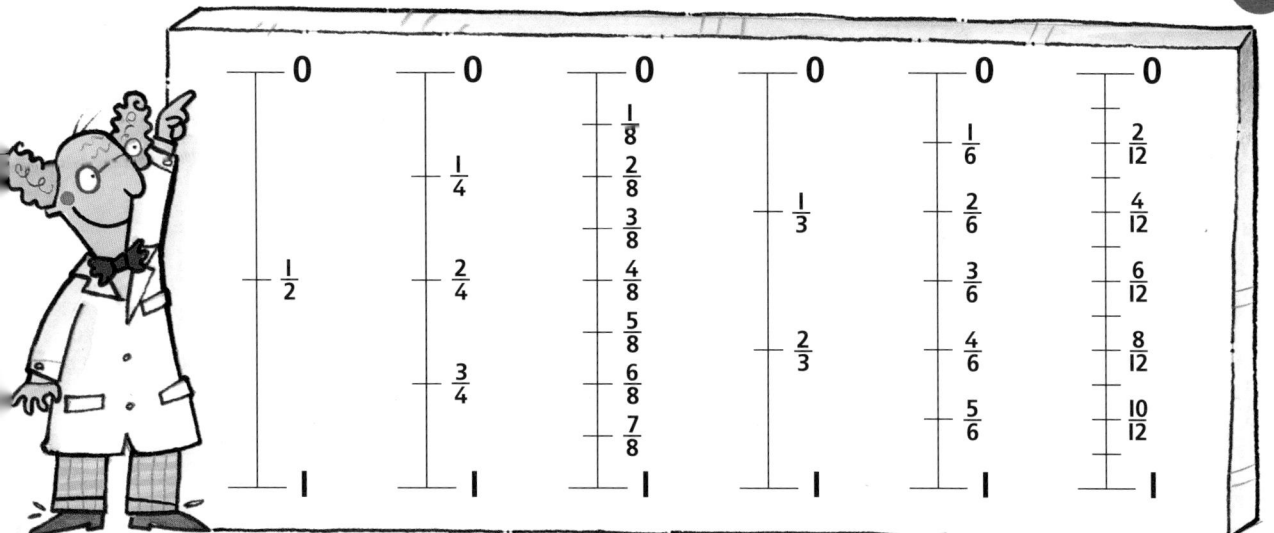

Copy and complete.

Use the fraction lines to help you.

1. $\dfrac{1}{2} = \dfrac{2}{4}$

1   $\dfrac{1}{2} = \dfrac{}{4}$

2   $\dfrac{1}{2} = \dfrac{4}{}$

3   $\dfrac{}{4} = \dfrac{2}{8}$

4   $\dfrac{1}{3} = \dfrac{2}{}$

5   $\dfrac{}{4} = \dfrac{6}{8}$

6   $\dfrac{1}{2} = \dfrac{}{6}$

7   $\dfrac{1}{3} = \dfrac{}{12}$

8   $\dfrac{2}{3} = \dfrac{4}{}$

9   $\dfrac{}{3} = \dfrac{8}{12}$

Write an equivalent fraction.

10    $\dfrac{4}{8}$

10. $\dfrac{4}{8} = \dfrac{1}{2}$

11   $\dfrac{6}{9}$

12   $\dfrac{4}{20}$

13   $\dfrac{3}{15}$

14   $\dfrac{1}{4}$

15   $\dfrac{4}{12}$

16   $\dfrac{1}{3}$

17   $\dfrac{1}{5}$

18   $\dfrac{4}{10}$

19   $\dfrac{12}{18}$

20   $\dfrac{8}{24}$

e   Write one more equivalent fraction for each.

Tenths and hundredths

Write how many tenths.

I  $\dfrac{60}{100}$

I. $\dfrac{60}{100} = \dfrac{6}{10}$

2  $\dfrac{30}{100}$　　3  $\dfrac{90}{100}$　　4  $\dfrac{10}{100}$　　5  $\dfrac{50}{100}$

6  $\dfrac{20}{100}$　　7  $\dfrac{40}{100}$　　8  $\dfrac{80}{100}$　　q  $\dfrac{70}{100}$

℮ Can you write any other equivalent fractions for any of these?

Write how many tenths of a litre.　Write how many hundredths of a litre.

10. $\dfrac{6}{10}\,l = \dfrac{60}{100}\,l$

10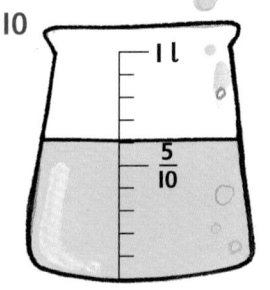

11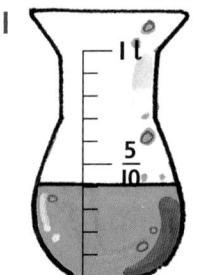

12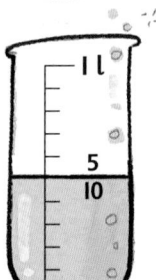

13

14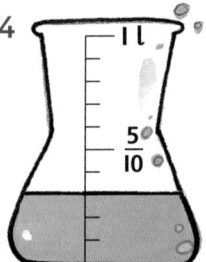

15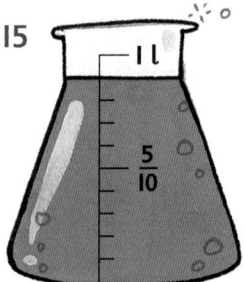

16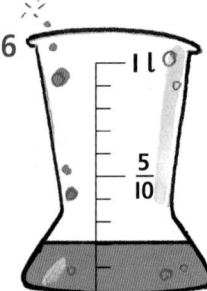

17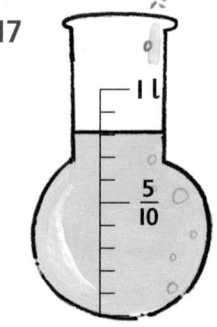

18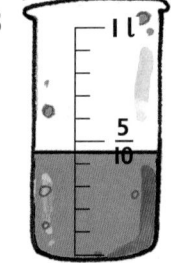

℮ Write each capacity in millilitres.

Equivalent fractions

Write an equivalent fraction with:

1a. $\dfrac{6}{8} = \dfrac{3}{4}$

1 denominator 4
- a $\dfrac{6}{8}$
- b $\dfrac{3}{12}$
- c $\dfrac{7}{2}$

2 numerator 1
- a $\dfrac{4}{8}$
- b $\dfrac{3}{12}$
- c $\dfrac{3}{9}$

3 denominator 10
- a $\dfrac{60}{100}$
- b $\dfrac{120}{100}$
- c $\dfrac{10}{100}$

4 denominator 2
- a $\dfrac{5}{10}$
- b $\dfrac{50}{100}$
- c $\dfrac{15}{10}$

e Write all the fractions in order, from smallest to largest.

Explore

Use number cards 1 to 20.

Arrange the cards to show fractions.

Make sets of equivalent fractions.

How many different sets can you make?

How many cards can you use in each set?

$\dfrac{1}{5}$ $\dfrac{2}{10}$ $\dfrac{3}{15}$ $\dfrac{4}{20}$

Fractions and division

Find the fraction of each amount.

1  $\frac{1}{4}$ of £36

1. $\frac{1}{4}$ of £ 3 6 = £ 9

2  $\frac{1}{5}$ of £50

3  $\frac{1}{10}$ of £250

4 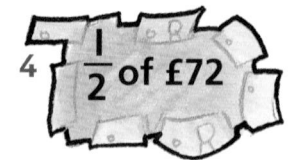 $\frac{1}{2}$ of £72

5  $\frac{1}{3}$ of £36

6 $\frac{1}{6}$ of £48

7  $\frac{1}{7}$ of £42

8 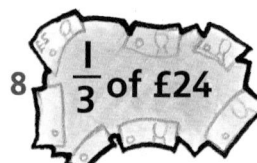 $\frac{1}{3}$ of £24

9 $\frac{1}{5}$ of £20

10 $\frac{1}{8}$ of £40

℮ Find $\frac{3}{4}$ of each original amount.

Copy and complete.

11 $\frac{1}{3}$ of 33 =

$\frac{1}{6}$ of 33 =

11. $\frac{1}{3}$ of 3 3 = 1 1

$\frac{1}{6}$ of 3 3 = 5 $\frac{1}{2}$

12 $\frac{1}{4}$ of 28 =

$\frac{1}{8}$ of 28 =

13 $\frac{1}{3}$ of 30 =

$\frac{1}{6}$ of 30 =

14 $\frac{1}{6}$ of 48 =

$\frac{1}{12}$ of 48 =

15 $\frac{1}{4}$ of 44 =

$\frac{1}{8}$ of 44 =

16 $\frac{1}{7}$ of 35 =

$\frac{1}{14}$ of 35 =

17 $\frac{1}{2}$ of 42 =

$\frac{1}{4}$ of 42 =

18 $\frac{1}{3}$ of 45 =

$\frac{1}{6}$ of 45 =

19 $\frac{1}{2}$ of 50 =

$\frac{1}{4}$ of 50 =

20 $\frac{1}{6}$ of 42 =

$\frac{1}{12}$ of 42 =

Fractions and division

Write how much each child must pay.

1
owes $\frac{3}{8}$
56p

I. $\frac{1}{8}$ of 5 6 p = 7 p

$\frac{3}{8}$ of 5 6 p = 2 1 p

2
owes $\frac{4}{5}$
40p

3
60p
owes $\frac{2}{3}$

4
owes $\frac{5}{6}$
72p

5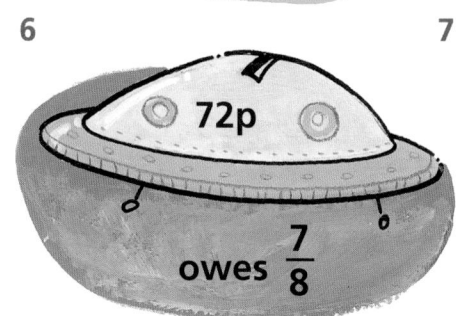
90p
owes $\frac{9}{10}$

6
72p
owes $\frac{7}{8}$

7
81p
owes $\frac{2}{3}$

Problems
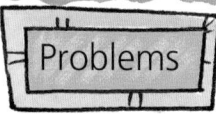

8 Asif takes £4·50 spending money on his school trip.

$\frac{1}{3}$ of this is his pocket money. How much does his mum give him?

9 James and Lily are collecting conkers. James has **35**.

Lily has $\frac{3}{5}$ that number.

How many more must she collect to have as many as James?

10 Clare's dad wants her to pay for $\frac{3}{4}$ of her new coat.

£24

How much does Clare owe him?

Fractions and division

Find how much is spent each time.

Start by halving.

1. $\frac{1}{4}$ £2·20

1. $\frac{1}{2}$ of £ 2·20 = £ 1·10

   $\frac{1}{4}$ of £ 2·20 = £ 0·55

2.  £4·20 $\frac{1}{4}$

3.  £3·40 $\frac{1}{4}$

4. £6·20 $\frac{1}{4}$

5.  £2·10 $\frac{1}{6}$

6.  £6·30 $\frac{1}{6}$

7. £10·50 $\frac{1}{6}$

8.  £4·40 $\frac{1}{8}$

9. £2·80 $\frac{1}{8}$

10.  £12·00 $\frac{1}{8}$

ℓ How much is left in each purse?

Explore

Work out these fractions of the numbers:

$\frac{1}{3}$ $\frac{1}{6}$ $\frac{1}{12}$

$\frac{1}{24}$ $\frac{1}{48}$

Making 100

> Write the pair to 100.

1  47

2  62

1. $4 7 + 5 3 = 1 0 0$

3  71

4  84

5  36

47 makes 100 → 60 → −10
47 makes 10 → 3
53

6  45

7  29

8  37

9 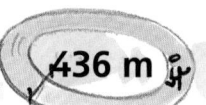 56

10  68

11 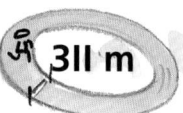 75

12 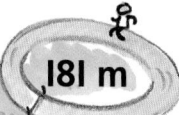 82

> Each lap is 100 m. Write how much further to the next lap.

13. $4 3 6 m + 6 4 m = 5 0 0 m$
    $6 4 m$ to next lap

13 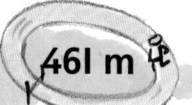 436 m

14 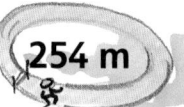 247 m

15 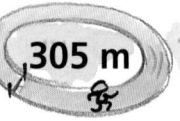 311 m

16 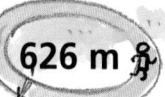 181 m

17  461 m

18 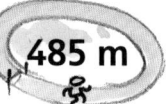 254 m

19 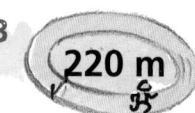 305 m

20  626 m

21  542 m

22  485 m

23  220 m

24 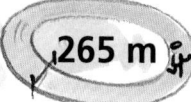 324 m

25 519 m

26 164 m

27 773 m

28 265 m

31

Making 1000

Write the pair to 1000.

1 **380**

1. $1000 - 380 = 620$

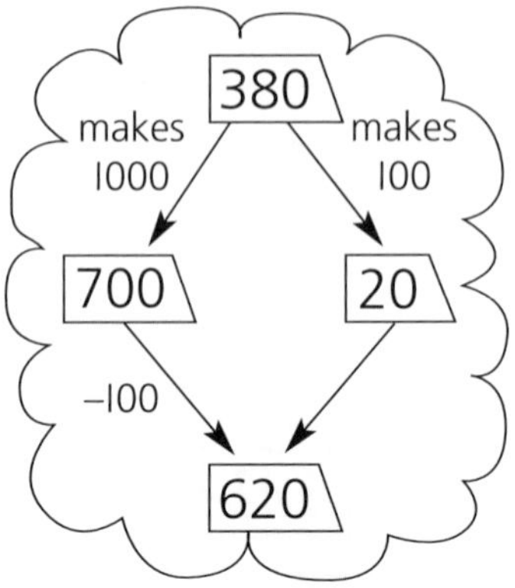

2 **420**

3 **350**

4 **110**

380

makes 1000   makes 100

700   20

−100

620

5 **250**

6 **450**

7 **640**

8 **330**

9 **750**

10 **840**

11 **650**

12 **520**

13 **480**

14 **610**

15 **850**

e Write a matching addition for each.

Each jigsaw has 500 pieces. How many pieces are missing?

16 **451 done**

16. $500 - 451 =$
   49 pieces

17 **412 done**

18 **432 done**

19 **484 done**

20 **446 done**

21 **478 done**

22 **424 done**

32

Making 100

> Each child has £100 in gift tokens. Write how much change they get.

1.  £72

1. £100 − £72 = £28

2  £48

3  £36

4  £83

5  £27

6  £94

7  £60

8  £51

9  £19

10  £75

Problems

11 Rachel has **64p**. She spends **20p** on a lolly. 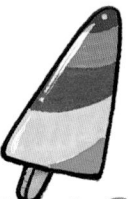 The bus home costs **£1**.  How much more does she need?

12 Ewan has cycled **52 km** already.  He cycles **24 km** further. How many more kilometres until he has cycled **100 km**?

13 Indira listened to her tape for **32** minutes.  She rewound the last **10** minutes.  How many minutes until the end of the **100** minute tape?

Adding several numbers

Write the total of the numbers to open each safe.

1. $5 + 7 + 8 + 3 + 9 = 3\ 2$

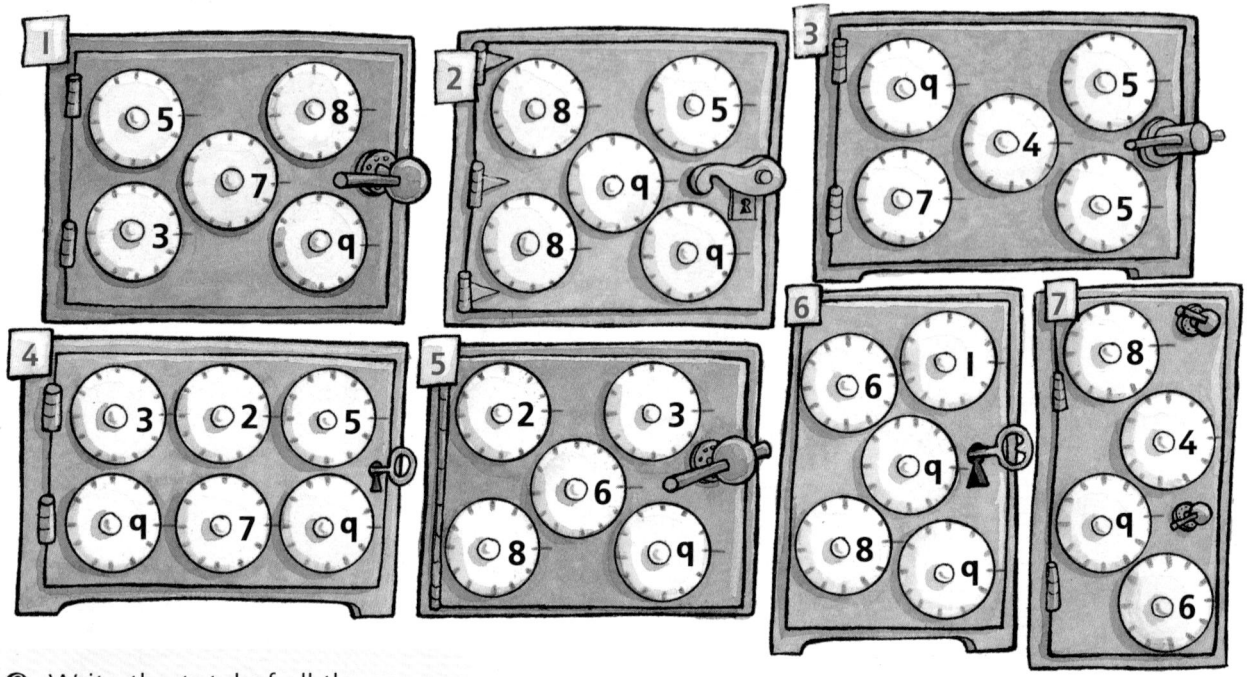

1. 5 8 7 3 9

2. 8 5 9 8 9

3. 9 5 4 7 5

4. 3 2 5 9 7 9

5. 2 3 6 8 9

6. 6 1 9 8 9

7. 8 4 9 6

● Write the total of all the scores.

Write how much in total.

8. £ 7 0 + £ 3 0 + £ 9 0 + £ 5 0 = £ 2 4 0

8 £90 £30 £70 £50

9 £60 £90 £40 £10

10 £70 £80 £90 £20

11 £10 £90 £30 £90

12 £50 £90 £20 £50

13 £90 £40 £60 £40

14 £90 £80 £30 £70

15 £20 £50 £80 £90

16 £50 £90 £30 £50

17 £90 £60 £20 £40

Adding several 2-digit numbers

Add the numbers.  54 + 29 + 36

1. $5 4 + 2 9 + 3 6 = 1 1 9$

Look for units which add to 10.

Look for near doubles.

To add 9, add 10 and take away 1.

2  39 + 72 + 28

4  24 + 49 + 36

6  34 + 29 + 36

8  72 + 18 + 9

10  64 + 23 + 36

3  17 + 43 + 29

5  45 + 28 + 35

7  27 + 25 + 39

9 24 + 46 + 38

11  17 + 26 + 43

e Write the nearest ten for each.

$1 9 + 9 1 = 1 1 0$

Find pairs which add to a multiple of 10.

 47

 26

82

45

 29

 34

19

23

 91

15

21

 78

Adding several multiples of 10

Write the perimeter of each frame.

1
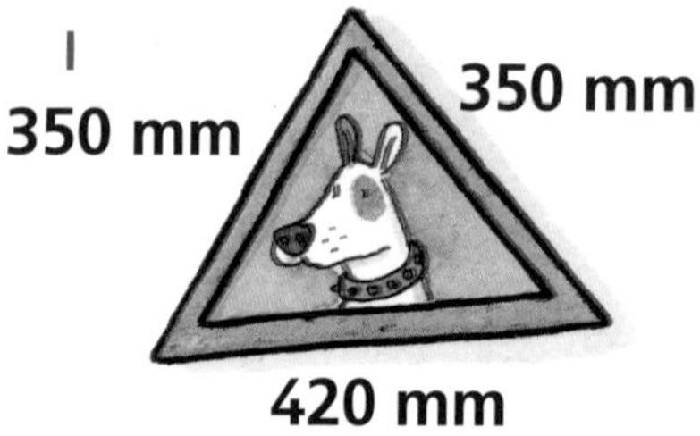
350 mm
350 mm
420 mm

1. 350 + 350 + 420 = 1120 mm

2
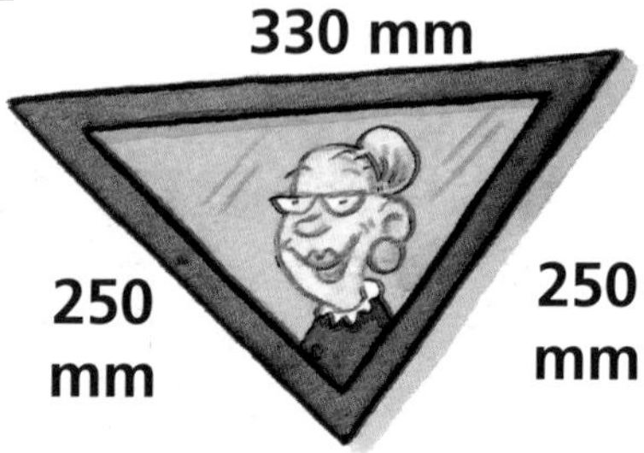
330 mm
250 mm
250 mm

3
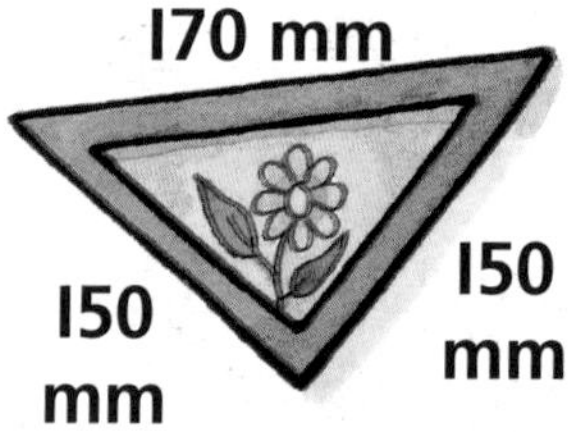
170 mm
150 mm
150 mm

4
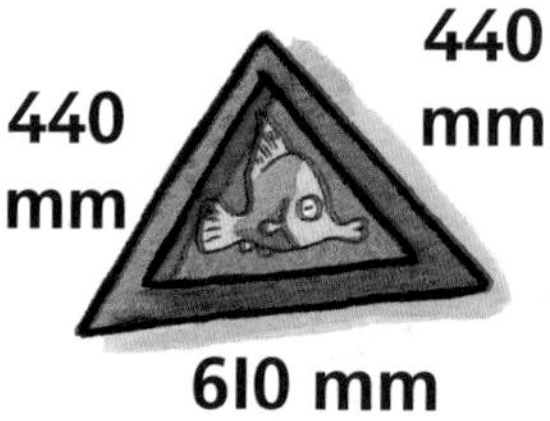
440 mm
440 mm
610 mm

5
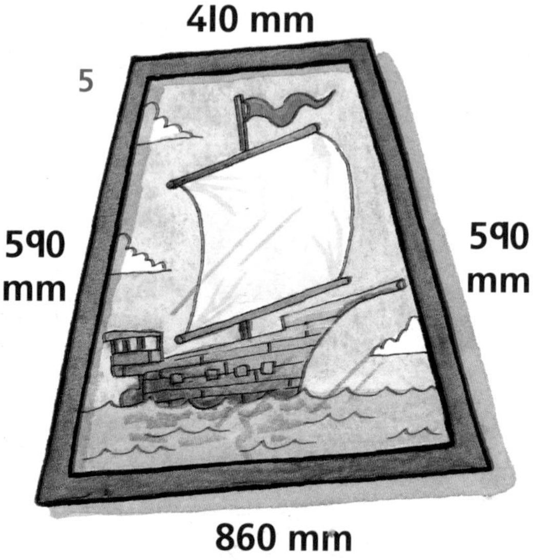
410 mm
590 mm
590 mm
860 mm

6
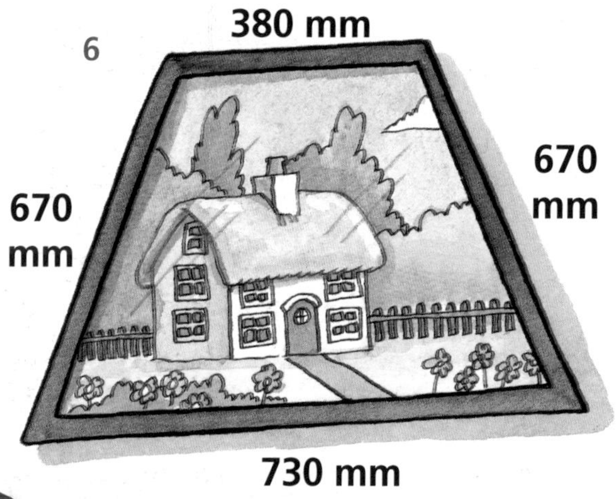
380 mm
670 mm
670 mm
730 mm

7
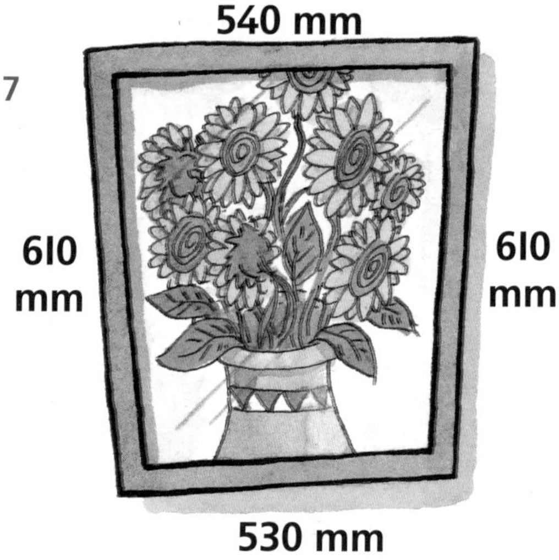
540 mm
610 mm
610 mm
530 mm

Explore

Write the consecutive odd numbers as shown.

Continue writing rows of odd numbers in the triangle.

Add each row.

What do you notice? Describe the pattern.

1
1 + 3
1 + 3 + 5
1 + 3 + 5 + 7
1 + 3 + 5 + 7 + 9
1 + ...

Adding several 2-digit numbers

Write how much each child's shopping costs.

1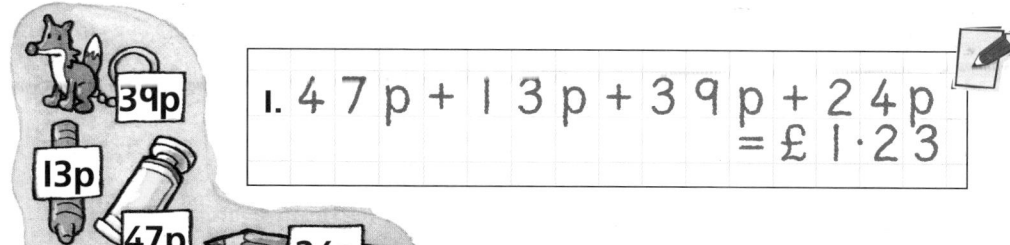

1. 4 7 p + 1 3 p + 3 9 p + 2 4 p
   = £ 1 · 2 3

2
28p 89p 32p 37p

3
43p 37p 28p 16p

4
54p 29p 36p 27p

5
69p 17p 48p 33p

6
25p 67p 43p 55p

7
94p 26p 35p 19p

8
61p 39p 18p 79p

9
32p 58p 29p 81p

10
64p 52p 19p 54p

⊜ How much change does each child get from £2?

11 Sameer had **48p**. He spent half of it.

His uncle gave him **66p**.

His mum gave him **75p** pocket money.

He bought an apple for **10p**.

How much does he have now?

Problems

12 The tape was **150 cm** long.

Kerry cut off **3** pieces.

One was **38 cm**.
One was **29 cm**.
One was **42 cm**.

How long is the tape now?

Copy and complete.   Estimate first.

I.

```
    8 0 0 0

      4 3 6 5
    + 4 4 7 8
          1 3
        1 3 0
        7 0 0
      8 0 0 0
      8 8 4 3
```

1
```
  4 3 6 5
+ 4 4 7 8
_____
```

2
```
  6 4 8 3
+ 2 5 9 8
_____
```

3
```
  4 5 9 6
+ 5 5 3 7
_____
```

4
```
  3 7 8 2
+ 4 3 3 5
_____
```

5
```
  6 5 2 4
+ 4 6 1 3
_____
```

6
```
  3 9 8 7
+ 8 3 1 5
_____
```

7
```
  9 5 1 6
+ 7 2 6 8
_____
```

Write each player's total score.

8.
```
    8 5 0 0

    4 5 6 5
  + 3 7 8 8
    8 3 5 3
    1 1 1
```

8
Game I: 4565
Game 2: 3788

9
Game I: 2034
Game 2: 6883

10
Game I: 4985
Game 2: 2925

11
Game I: 4136
Game 2: 5721

12
Game I: 6005
Game 2: 7146

13
Game I: 8259
Game 2: 4061

14
Game I: 2074
Game 2: 5999

🍂 In the third game each player scores 2715 points. Write the total scores now.

Adding two 4-digit numbers

Write how many tickets were sold in total for each match.

1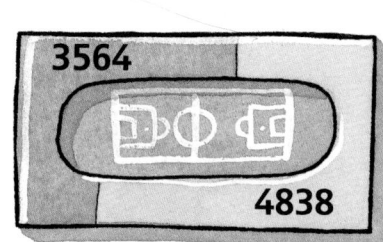
3564
4838

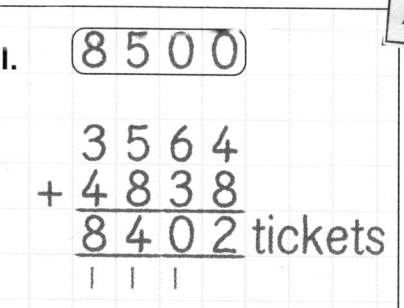
1. 8500

  3 5 6 4
+ 4 8 3 8
  8 4 0 2 tickets
  I I I

2
6092
1873

3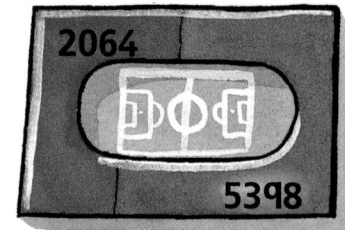
2064
5398

4
7344
3684

5
4617
4988

6
2773
6319

7
8246
6532

8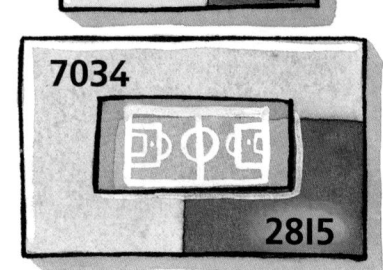
7034
2815

9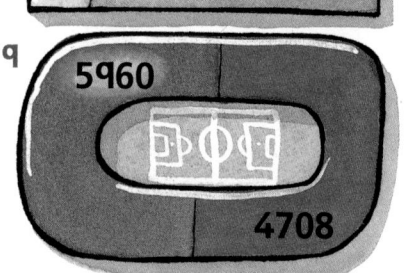
5960
4708

10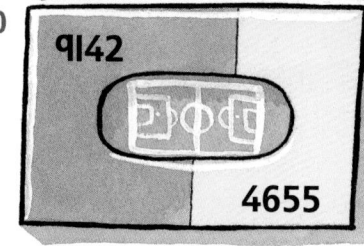
9142
4655

e Each ground has 15 000 seats. How many seats were empty?

Explore

Turn these numbers into palindromes (a number that is the same when you reverse its digits).

168

364

192

553

| Choose a number. |
| Reverse its digits. |
| Add the numbers together. |
| Is it a palindrome? |
| Yes | No |

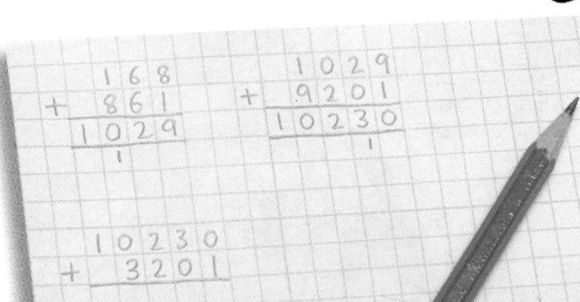

Write the total number of people in each area.

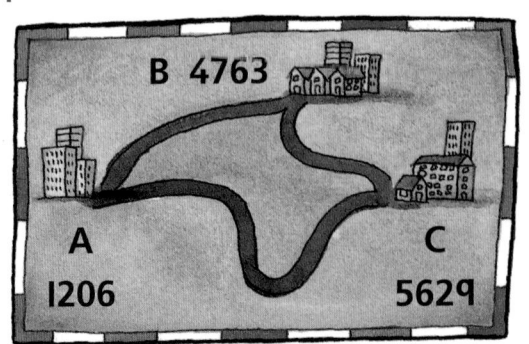

B 4763

A 1206

C 5629

I.

```
  1 1 5 0 0

    4 7 6 3
    5 6 2 9
+   1 2 0 6
  1 1 5 9 8
    1     1
```

2 D 3617
   E 4829
   F 6018

3 G 8275
   H 3368
   I 4237

4 J 8104
   K 2799
   L 4081

5 M 5546
   N 2911
   O 1769

6 P 3427
   Q 4618
   R 9258

7 S 9699
   T 5806
   U 8173

@ 896 people move to each area. What is the new population?

Problems

8 An aeroplane flies **3242** miles on Sunday.

It flies **3689** miles on Monday and **2965** miles on Tuesday. How far has the plane flown?

The plane flies **12 000** miles in a week.

How much further does it fly?

9 A greengrocer earns **£4765** in the first quarter of the year.

He earns **£3691** in the second quarter and **£2815** in the third.

In the last quarter he earns **£2249**. How much does he earn in the whole year?

Counting in steps of different sizes

Write the next 4 numbers.

I. 2 0 0, 2 5 0, 3 0 0, 3 5 0

1 0 50 100 150

2 0 25 50 75

3 950 900 850 800

4 725 750 775 800

5 625 600 575 550

6 0 30 60 90

7 0 9 18 27

8 118 125 132 139

9 320 380 440 500

10 99 91 83 75

ℓ Write the 2 numbers before.

11 410 370 330 290

Write the numbers which are multiples of 25.

Which are multiples of 50? Of 5? Of 10?

3665

2625

4010

1084

1050

1250

1333

3775

8235

5551

41

Write the position of the finger on each stick.

1. 4 4

1

0 — 110

2

0 — 90

3

0 — 80

4

0 — 120

5

0 — 200

6

0 — 250

7

0 — 190

8

0 — 170

Write the next 4 numbers.

9 0 15 30 45

9. 6 0, 7 5, 9 0, 1 0 5

10 150 135 120

11 0 60 120 180

12 240 200 160

13 0 12 24 36

14 96 108 120

15 900 945 990

Sequences

The fleas make equal jumps along the number lines.

Write the first eight numbers they land on.

ı. 8, 3 3, 5 8, 8 3, ...

Finbar Flea jumps in 25s.

1
| 0 | 8 | 10 |

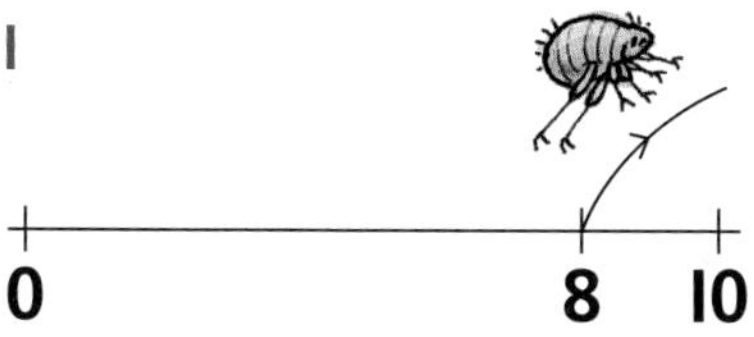

2
| 10 | 13 | 20 |

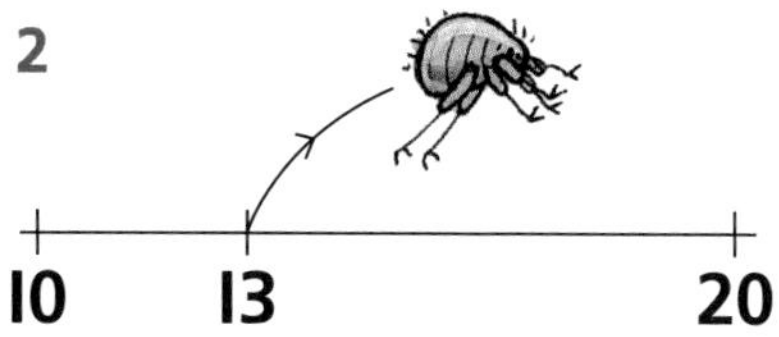

3
| 20 | 22 | 30 |

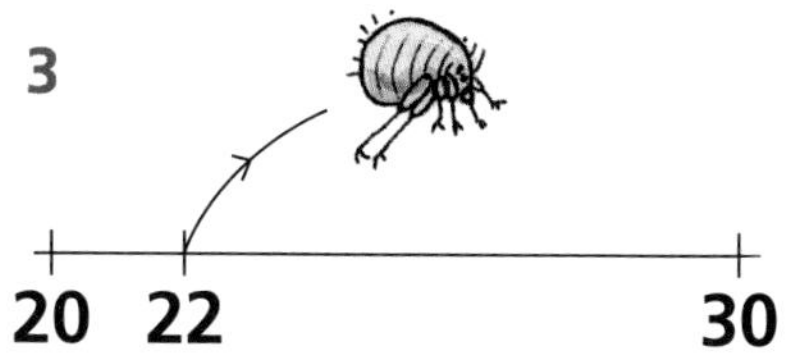

Fiona Flea jumps in 50s.

4
| 10 | 16 | 20 |

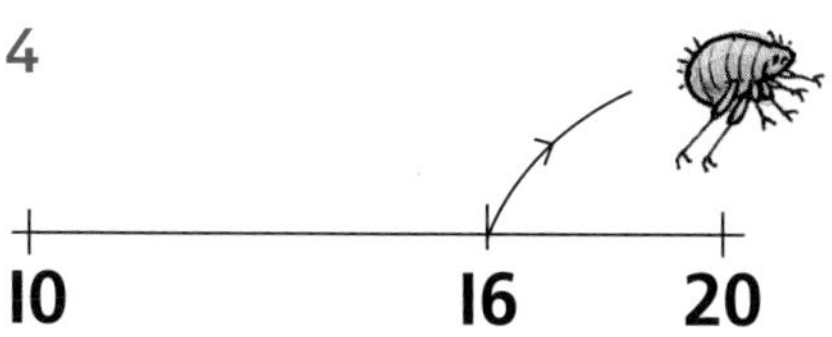

5
| 10 | 12 | 20 |

6
| 40 | 44 | 50 |

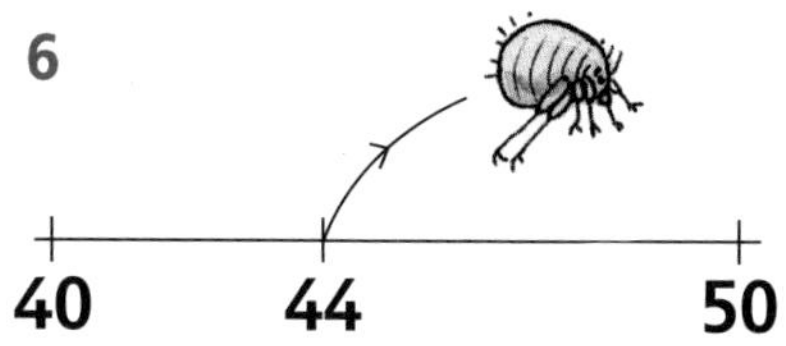

Fitzroy Flea jumps in 21s.

7
| 0 | 10 |

8
| 30 | 32 | 40 |

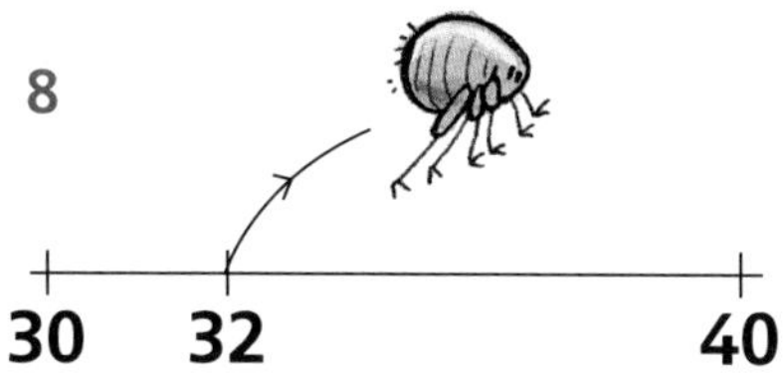

q
| 40 | 47 | 50 |

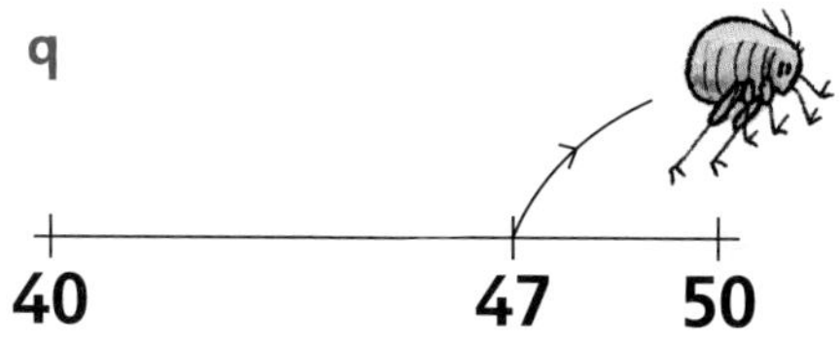

Faith Flea jumps in 18s.

10
| 0 | 10 |

11
| 30 | 35 | 40 |

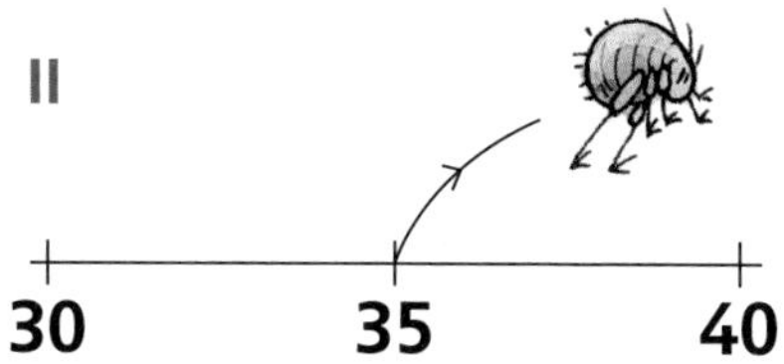

12 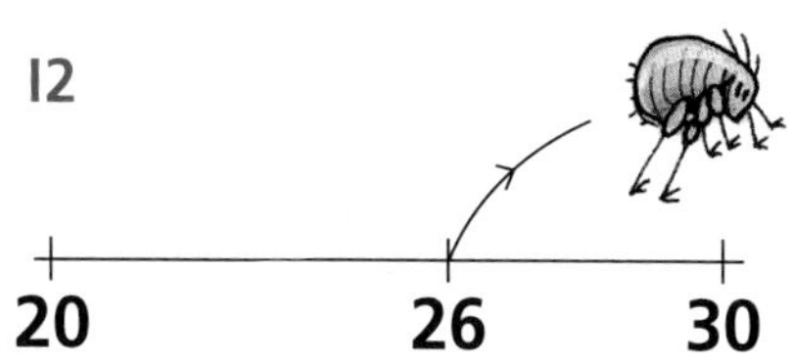
| 20 | 26 | 30 |

e Each flea starts at 1000 and jumps back. Write the first four numbers they land on.

Explore

Write the first ten multiples of 15.

Write the units digits. What is the pattern?

Explore patterns in the units digits of multiples of other numbers, e.g. 19, 17, ...

15, 30, 45, 60, 75

Write the first ten multiples for each number.

Write the common multiples for each pair.

1. multiples of 2: 2, 4, 6, 8, 1 0, 1 2, 1 4, 1 6, 1 8, 2 0

multiples of 5: 5, 1 0, 1 5, 2 0, 2 5, 3 0, 3 5, 4 0, 4 5, 5 0

common multiples: 1 0, 2 0

1. 2 and 5

2. 3 and 4

3. 2 and 3

4. 4 and 5

5. 5 and 3

6. 10 and 15

7. 20 and 30

8. 20 and 25

Write three numbers which have these common multiples.

Use the multiplication square to help you.

9. 2, 3, 4

9. 12

10. 18

11. 16

12. 20

13. 6

14. 30

15. 42

16. 40

17. 32

18. 36

1	2	3	4	5	6	7	8	9	10
2	4	6	8	10	12	14	16	18	20
3	6	9	12	15	18	21	24	27	30
4	8	12	16	20	24	28	32	36	40
5	10	15	20	25	30	35	40	45	50
6	12	18	24	30	36	42	48	54	60
7	14	21	28	35	42	49	56	63	70
8	16	24	32	40	48	56	64	72	80
9	18	27	36	45	54	63	72	81	90
10	20	30	40	50	60	70	80	90	100

Copy this grid.

Colour the multiples of 2.

Colour the multiples of 3.

Describe the pattern of the common multiples of 2 and 3.

1	2	3	4	5	6	7
8	9	10	11	12	13	14
15	16	17	18	19	20	21
22	23	24	25	26	27	28
29	30	31	32	33	34	35
36	37	38	39	40	41	42
43	44	45	46	47	48	49

Some numbers will be coloured twice.

Repeat for this grid.

Colour the multiples of 4 and 5.

Describe the pattern of the common multiples of 4 and 5.

1	2	3	4	5	6	7	8	9	10
11	12	13	14	15	16	17	18	19	20
21	22	23	24	25	26	27	28	29	30
31	32	33	34	35	36	37	38	39	40
41	42	43	44	45	46	47	48	49	50

Explore

Draw a 9 × 9 grid.

Describe the pattern of the common multiples of 2 and 5.

Find other pairs of numbers which have common multiples that make a pattern.

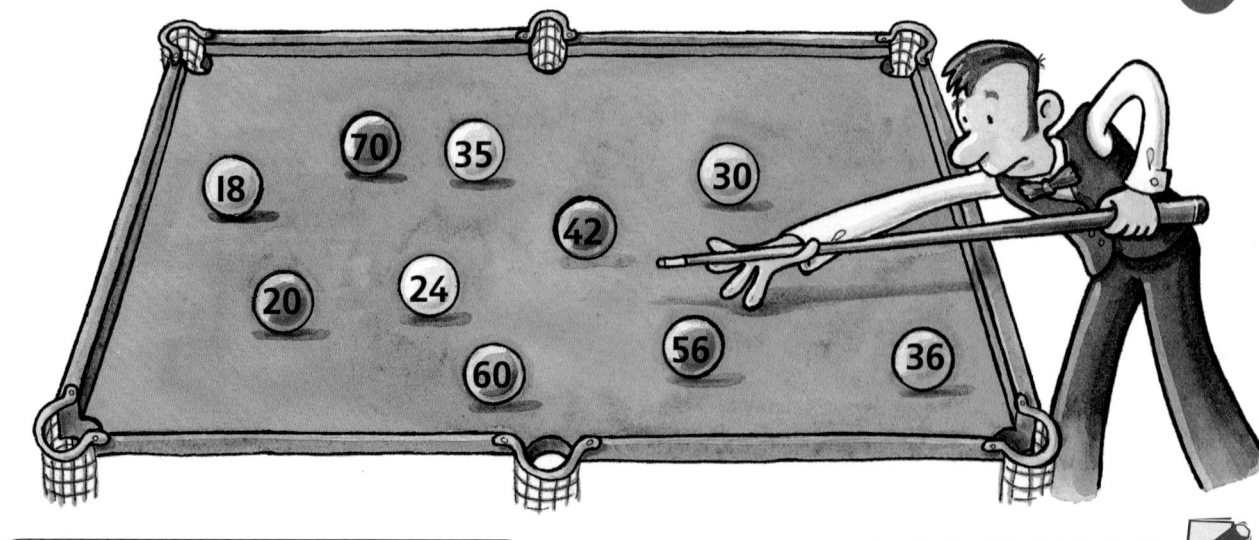

Write which numbers on the balls are common multiples of:

I. 1 8, 2 4, 3 0,
   3 6, 4 2, 6 0

1 2 and 3

2 4 and 5

3 5 and 7

4 3 and 6

5 4 and 6

6 2 and 9

7 6 and 7

8 7 and 8

9 5 and 15

e Which number is a common multiple of 2, 3, 4, 5 and 6?

10 I am a multiple of 2.
    I am a multiple of 3.
    I am between 15 and 20.

11 I am a multiple of 2.
    I am a multiple of 7.
    I am less than 15.

12 I am a common
    multiple of 2, 3 and 5.
    I am between 80 and 100.

Who am I?

13 I am a 2-digit number.
    I am a common
    multiple of 2 and 3.
    I am less than 15.

14 I am a common multiple
    of 3, 4 and 5. I am not
    60. I am less than 150.

15 I am a common
    multiple of 10 and 15.
    I am between 70 and 100.

Write how many 10p pieces in each amount.

1  £637

1. $637 \times 10 = 6370$

2  £491

3 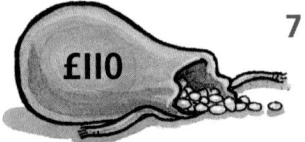 £276

4  £535

5  £860

6  £110

7  £308

8  £940

9  £719

10 £2670

11 £5300

12 £4106

13 £2700

Write how many 1p pieces in each amount.

1a. $637 \times 100 = 63{,}700$

Write the missing numbers.

14. $43 \times 100 = 4300$

14 $43 \times$ 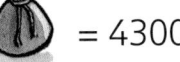 $= 4300$

15 $10 \times$  $= 190$

16 $72 \times 100 =$

17 $38 \times$  $= 380$

18 $52 \times$  $= 5200$

19 $\times 100 = 6400$

20 $84 \times$ $\times 10 = 8400$

21 $10 \times 61 \times 10 =$

Dividing by 10 and 100

Write how many £10 notes are needed to buy each item.

1
£230

I. £ 2 3 0 ÷ £ 1 0 = 2 3

2
£460

3
£540

4
£1220

5
£640

6
£7120

7
£890

8
£2060

9
£3120

10
£5950

11
£780

12
£930

13
£2730

How many 10p coins would you need to pay for each?

Write how many times the larger number must be divided by 10 to make the smaller number.

14.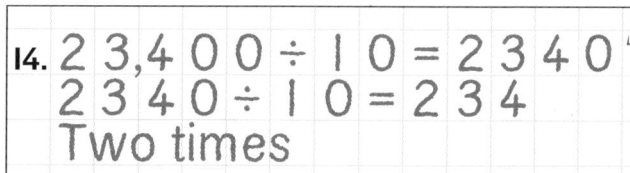
2 3,4 0 0 ÷ 1 0 = 2 3 4 0
2 3 4 0 ÷ 1 0 = 2 3 4
Two times

14
23 400
234

15
891 000
891

16
72 400
724

17
31 000
31

18
2700
27

19
636 000
6360

20
12 400
1240

21
56 200
562

22
965 000
96 500

Multiplying and dividing decimals by 10 and 100

> Each baby creature grows to 10 times its length.

> How long is each now?

> I. $0.5 \text{ cm} \times 10 = 5 \text{ cm}$

1
0.5 cm

2
0.3 cm

3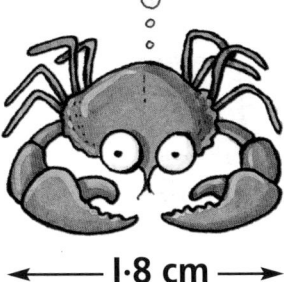
1.8 cm

4
0.7 cm

5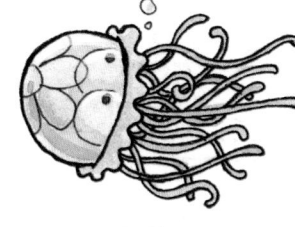
0.2 cm

6
2.9 cm

7
6.1 cm

8
5.6 cm

9
7.4 cm

e How long would each creature be if it grew to 100 times its first length?

> Copy and complete.

10 $27 \div 10 =$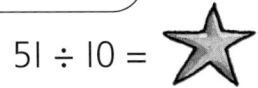

> 10. $27 \div 10 = 2.7$

11 $51 \div 10 =$

12 $620 \div 100 =$ ⭐

13 $840 \div 100 =$ ⭐

14 $96 \div$ ⭐ $= 9.6$

15 $710 \div 100 =$ ⭐

16 $590 \div$ ⭐ $= 5.9$

17 $370 \div$ ⭐ $= 3.7$

18 ⭐ $\div 10 = 6.8$

19 ⭐ $\div 100 = 4.3$

1 × 7 = 7	1 × 8 = 8	1 × 9 = 9
2 × 7 = 14	2 × 8 = 16	2 × 9 = 18
3 × 7 = 21	3 × 8 = 24	3 × 9 = 27
4 × 7 = 28	4 × 8 = 32	4 × 9 = 36
5 × 7 = 35	5 × 8 = 40	5 × 9 = 45
6 × 7 = 42	6 × 8 = 48	6 × 9 = 54
7 × 7 = 49	7 × 8 = 56	7 × 9 = 63
8 × 7 = 56	8 × 8 = 64	8 × 9 = 72
9 × 7 = 63	9 × 8 = 72	9 × 9 = 81
10 × 7 = 70	10 × 8 = 80	10 × 9 = 90

Use doubling to complete the multiplication facts.

1 8 × 18

1. 8 × 18 = 144

2 6 × 14   3 5 × 16   4 9 × 14   5 3 × 18   6 7 × 16

7 4 × 16   8 9 × 18   9 8 × 14   10 5 × 18   11 3 × 16

ℯ Write the ×14, ×16 and ×18 tables.

Use the tables above and doubling to write the missing numbers.

12 3 × 28 =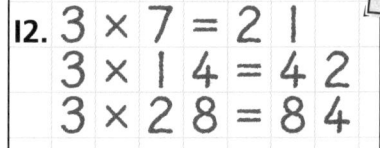

12. 3 × 7 = 21
3 × 14 = 42
3 × 28 = 84

13 6 × 28 = 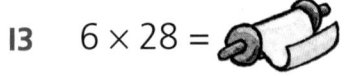   14 4 × 32 =   15 2 × 36 =

16 7 × 32 =   17 8 × 28 =   18 7 × 36 =

19 5 × 28 =   20 3 × 36 =   21 6 × 32 =

22 9 × 32 =   23 7 × 28 =   24 9 × 36 =

Multiplying by doubling and halving

Write the missing numbers.

1. $16 \times 45 = 8 \times 90$
   $= 720$

1   $16 \times 45 = 8 \times$  $=$

2   $12 \times 35 = 6 \times$  $=$

3   $8 \times 45 =$  $\times 90 =$

4   $18 \times 25 =$ 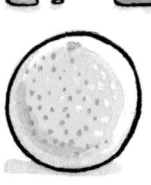 $\times 50 =$

5   $14 \times 15 =$ 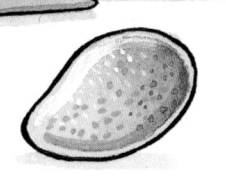 $\times$ 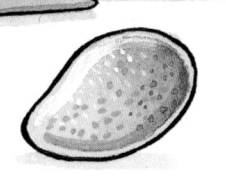 $=$

6   $6 \times 55 = 3$ $\times$ $=$

apples 15p each	oranges 25p each	coconuts 45p each	grapefruits 35p each	mangoes 55p each

Write the total cost of:

Use doubling and halving.

7. $18 \times 15p = 9 \times 30p$
   $= 270p$
   $= £2·70$

7   18 apples

8   16 grapefruits

9   14 mangoes

10   18 oranges

11   12 coconuts

12   16 apples

13   14 coconuts

14   8 oranges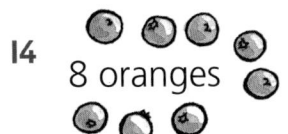

15   12 grapefruits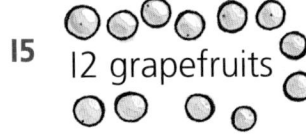

Groups of children are going on a train journey.

Write the total cost for each group.

I. $8 \times £3.50 = 4 \times £7$
$= £28$

Use doubling and halving.

1 TICKET **£3·50**

8 children

2 TICKET **£4·50**

12 children

3 TICKET **£1·50**

14 children

4 TICKET **£3·25**

16 children

5 TICKET **£1·25**

16 children

6 TICKET **£4·25**

8 children

7 TICKET **£1·10**

12 children

8 TICKET **£3·20**

16 children

9 TICKET **£4·15**

8 children

e Find the total cost if a class of 32 children goes on each trip.

Explore

Sometimes you can multiply by continuing to halve and double. Use this method to find:

 8 × 22    16 × 21   32 × 15

Choose some of your own numbers and multiply them by 8, 16, 32 or 64. Check with a calculator.

16 × 25
= 8 × 50
= 4 × 100
= 2 × 200
= 1 × 400
= **400**

32 × 14
= 16 × 28
= 8 × 56
= 4 × 112
= 2 × 224
= 1 × 448
= **448**

Multiplying

The vehicles use the same amount of petrol each week.

Write how much each uses in 8 weeks.

1. $8 \times 23 \cdot 5\,l = 4 \times 47\,l$
   $= 2 \times 94\,l$
   $= 188\,l$

1

23·5 l

2

43·5 l

3

34·25 l

4

16·5 l

5

21·25 l

6

56·5 l

7

9·25 l

8

35·5 l

9

29·25 l

Problems

10 Sasha watches a TV programme for **1** hour.

There are **4** commercial breaks every hour, each **3½** minutes long.

How long is the programme?

11 Jason buys **6** video tapes.

Each tape costs **£1·25**.

How much change does he get from **£10**?

12 Hattie records some songs onto a tape.

8 songs are **4·5** minutes long.

12 songs are **3·5** minutes long.

How long is left on a **90** minute tape?

Multiplying by 5 and 50

Doughnuts are packed in boxes of 5.

Write how many are ordered for each party.

I. 18 × 10 = 180
18 × 5 = 90

1
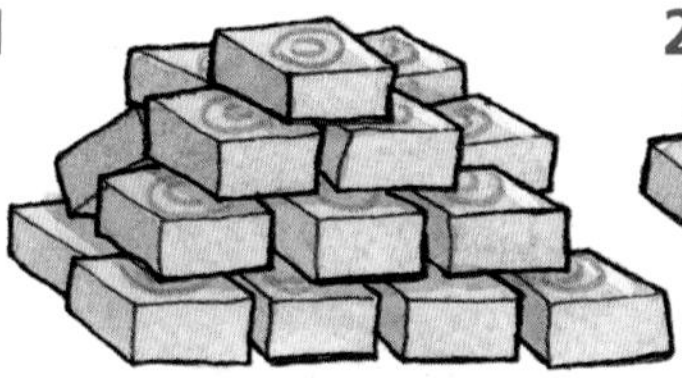
18 boxes

2
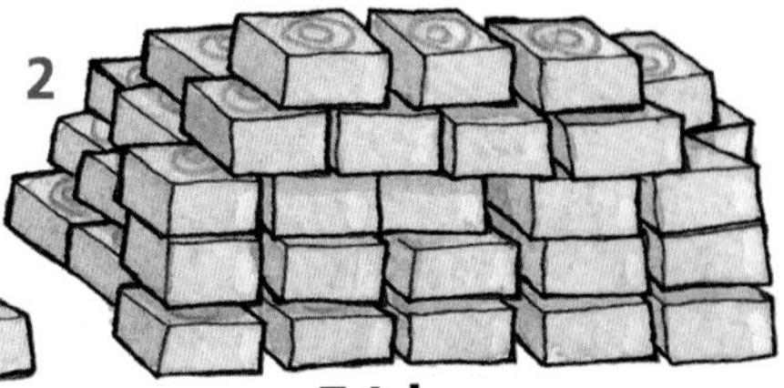
54 boxes

3
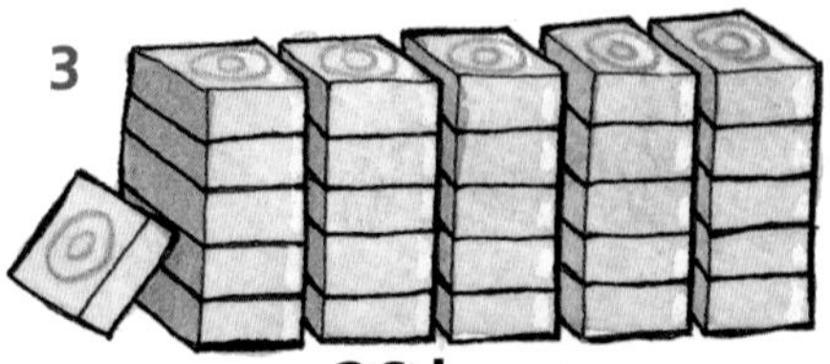
26 boxes

4
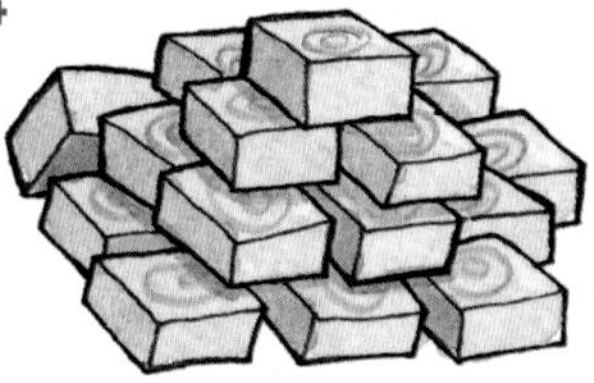
19 boxes

5
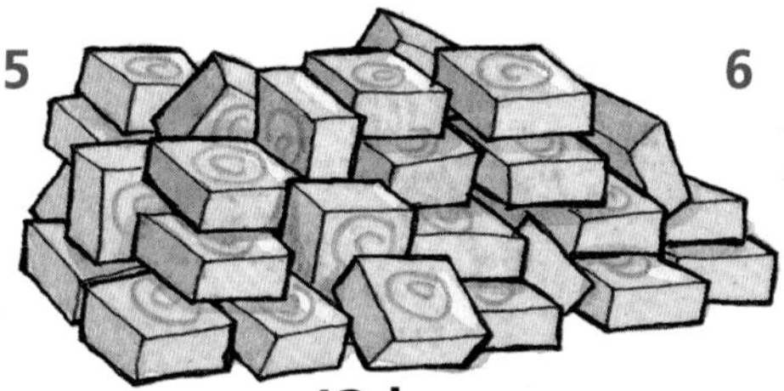
43 boxes

6
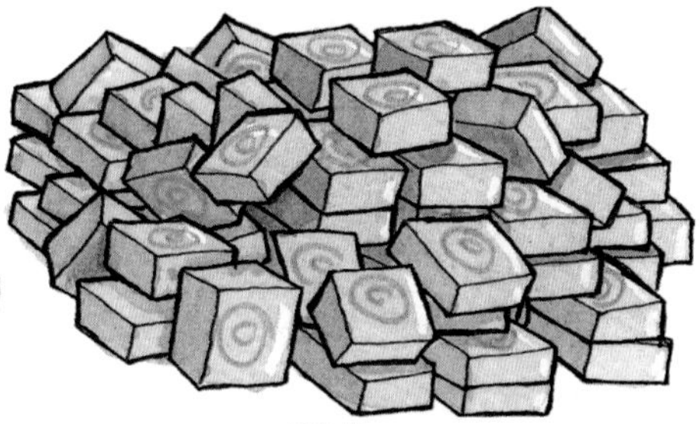
61 boxes

7
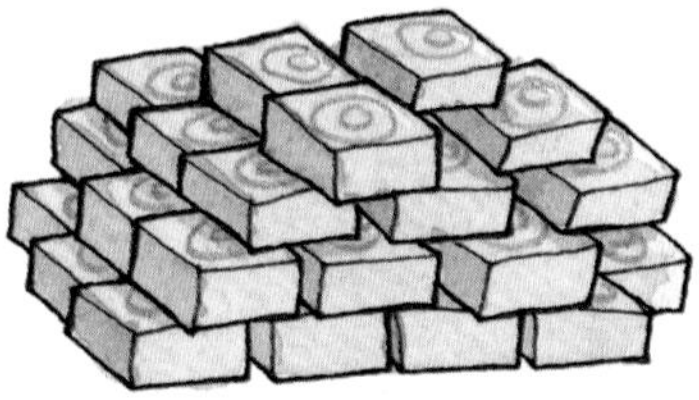
35 boxes

8
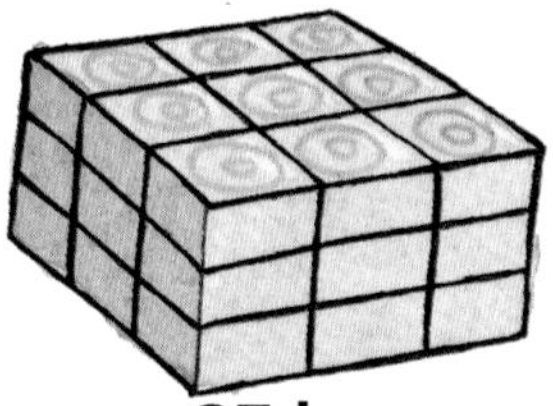
27 boxes

9
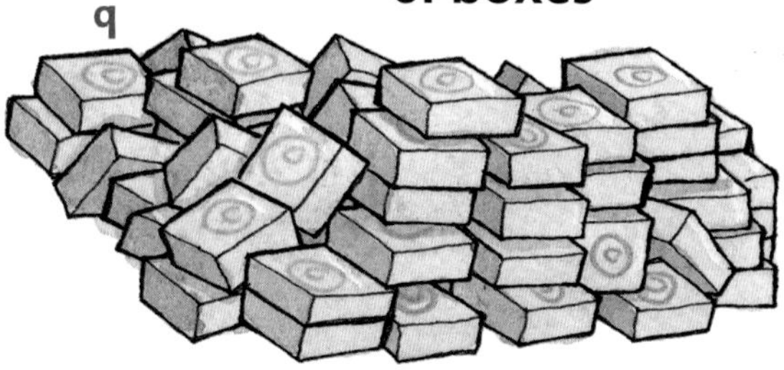
57 boxes

How many boxes of doughnuts are needed if they are packed in boxes of 4?

Copy and complete.

10 42 × 50 =

10. 42 × 100 = 4200
42 × 50 = 2100

11 66 × 50 =

12 50 × 84 =

13 50 × 48 =

14 45 × 50 =

15 50 × 27 =

16 19 × 50 =

17 146 × 50 =

18 50 × 216 =

19 50 × 170 =

Multiplying by 5 and 50

Each matchbox contains 50 matches.

Write how many matches.

1. $24 \times 100 = 2400$
$24 \times 50 = 1200$

1
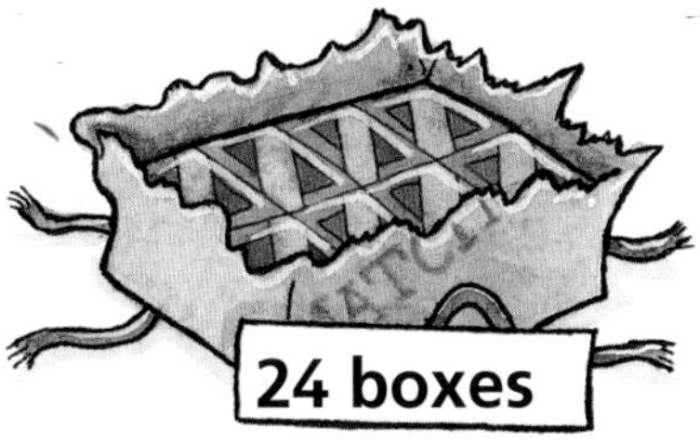
24 boxes

2
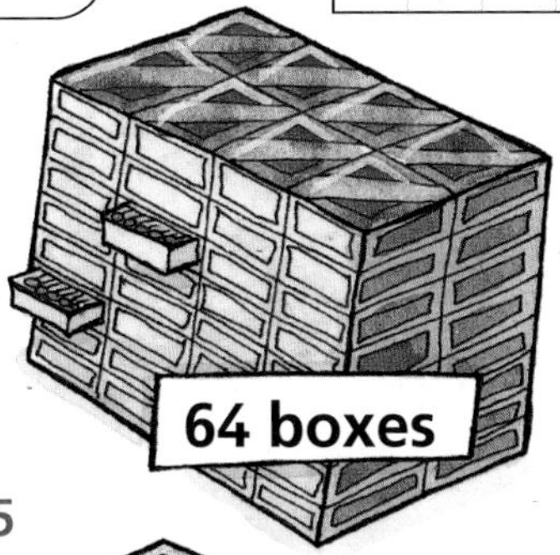
64 boxes

3
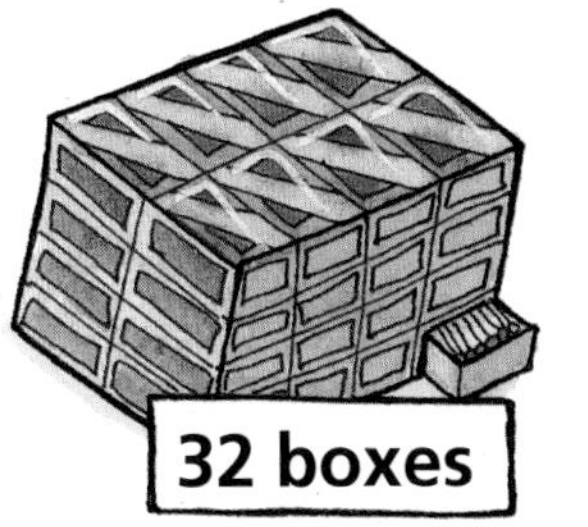
32 boxes

4
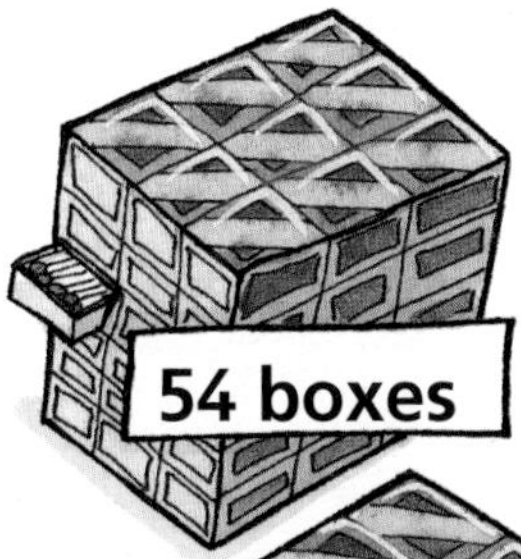
54 boxes

5
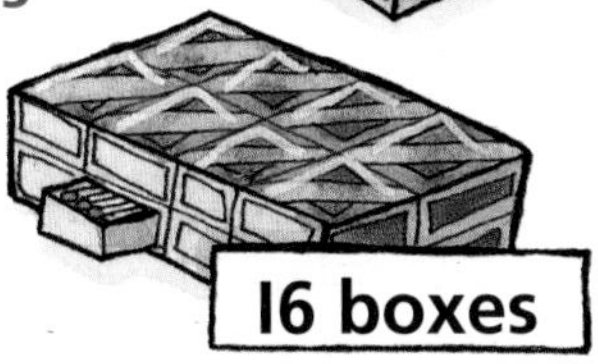
16 boxes

6
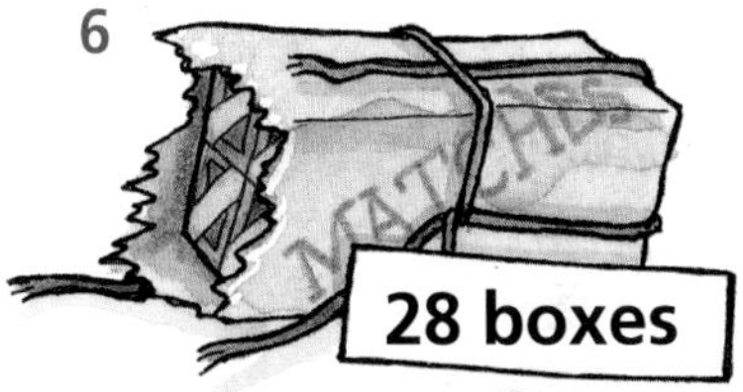
28 boxes

7
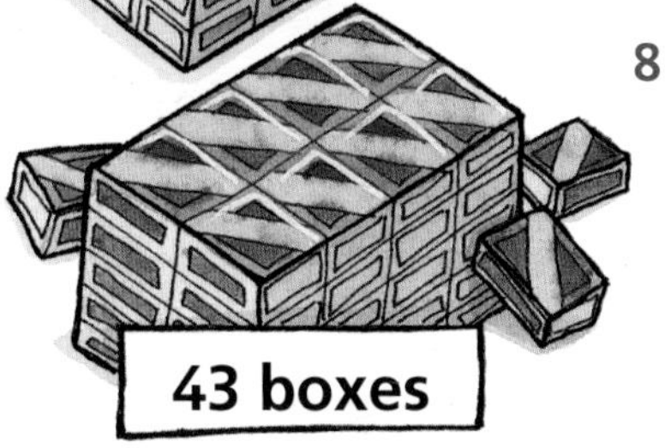
43 boxes

8
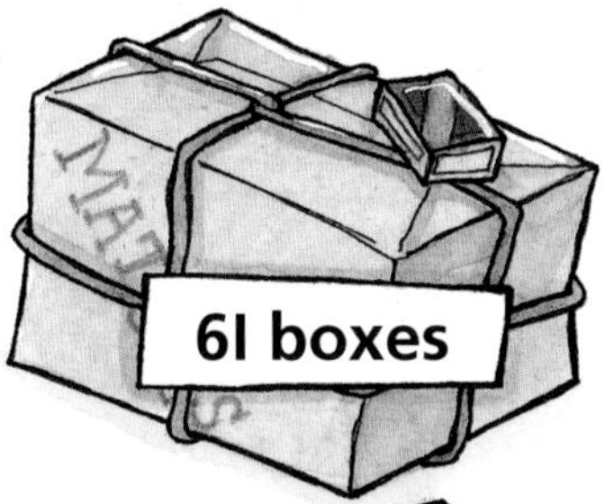
61 boxes

9
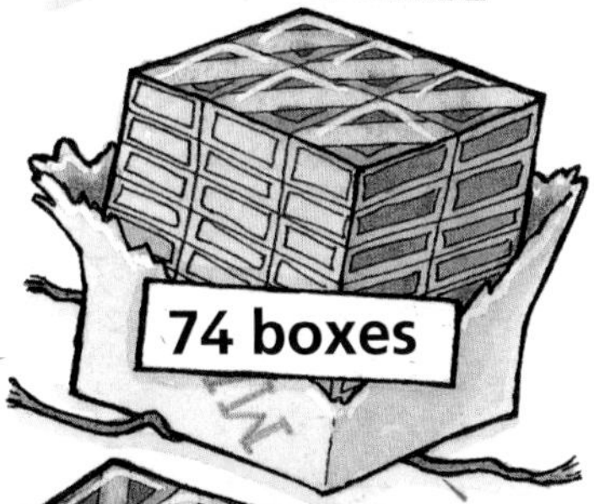
74 boxes

10
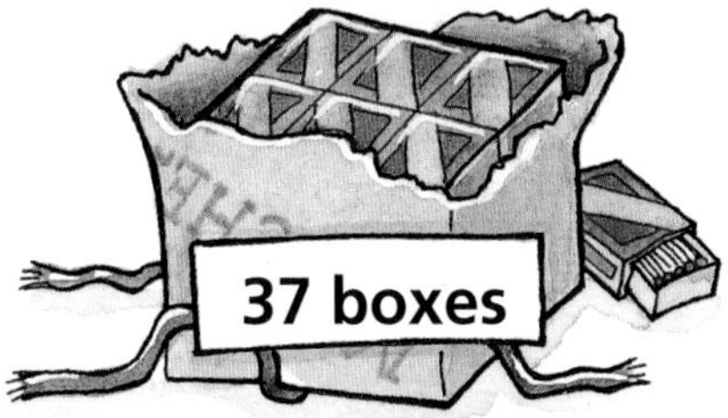
37 boxes

11
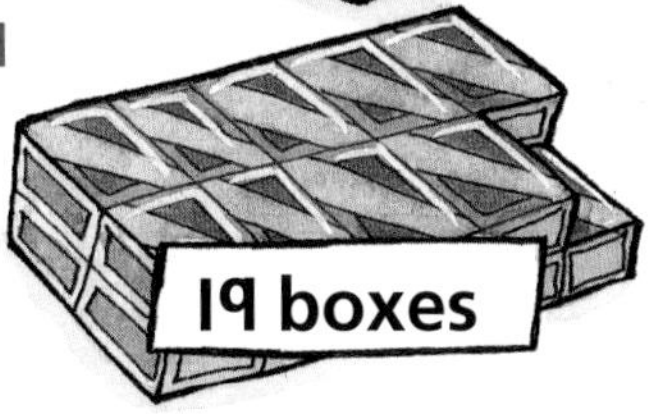
19 boxes

12
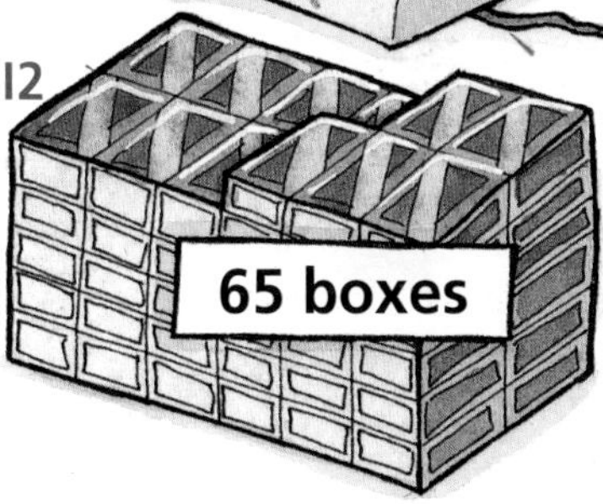
65 boxes

Explore

Dion has saved £84 in bags of 5p coins and bags of 50p coins.

Each bag contains exactly 20 coins.

How many bags could he have?

Work out how much each bag must be worth.

50p
5p

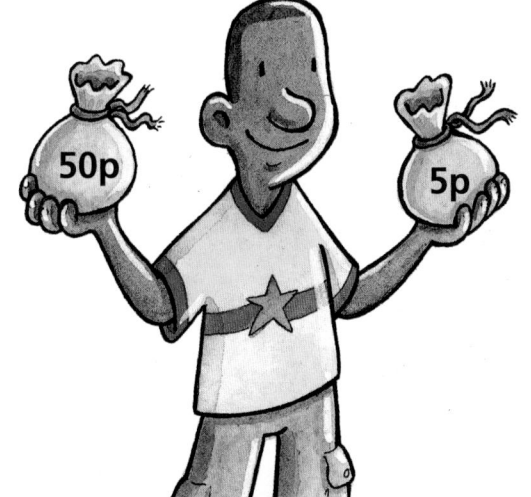

Multiplying by 5, 25 and 50

> Score 25 points for each hit.

> Write how many points in total.

```
I. 44 × 100 = 4400
   44 × 50 = 2200
   44 × 25 = 1100
```

I
44 hits

2
84 hits

3
24 hits

4
68 hits

5
54 hits

6
32 hits

7
16 hits

8
28 hits

q
48 hits

e How many points if each hit scores 12·5 points?

10 Each week Mike saves a **5p** coin and Kirsten saves a **50p** coin.
How much will they each have after a year?

II Rides on a roundabout cost **5p**. A class of **32** children each have a ride.
How much change from **£2** will there be?

Problems

12 Ella is sending **25** party invitations.
Each envelope needs a **27p** stamp.
How much will it cost to post the invitations?

13 A mystery number is multiplied by **50**.
The answer is **1200**.
What is the mystery number?

Multiplying

20p **30p** **40p** **50p** **60p** **70p**

Write the cost of these fish.

1

1. $7 \times 20p = 140p$
   $= £1.40$

2

3

4

5

6

7

8

9

10

℮ How many of each fish can be bought with £5?

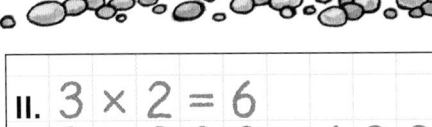
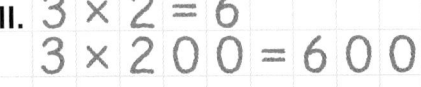

Copy and complete.

11 $3 \times 200 =$

11. $3 \times 2 = 6$
    $3 \times 200 = 600$

12 $3 \times 300 =$

13 $4 \times 600 =$

14 $5 \times 400 =$

15 $2 \times 700 =$

16 $5 \times 300 =$

17 $600 \times 3 =$

18 $7 \times 600 =$

19 $500 \times 8 =$

20 $3 \times 900 =$

57

Write the cost of each holiday.

1
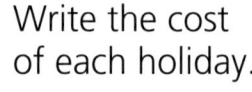
2 adults to Mexico

1. $2 \times 6 = 12$
   $2 \times £600 = £1200$

2
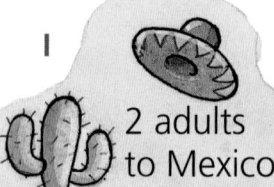
4 adults to Spain

3

5 adults to Italy

4

3 adults to Dubai

5
2 adults and 2 children to Florida

6

1 adult and 2 children to Mexico

7
3 adults and 3 children to France

A family of 2 adults and 2 children have saved £5000.

How much spending money would they have in each country?

Multiplying

> Write how many chocolate bars each factory makes.

1. $2 \times 600 = 1200$
   $20 \times 600 = 12,000$

1 20 hours
   600 bars an hour

2 30 hours
   500 bars an hour

3 40 hours
   300 bars an hour

4 50 hours
   200 bars an hour

5 30 hours
   400 bars an hour

6 50 hours
   300 bars an hour

> Copy and complete.

7 $30 \times 400 =$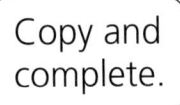

7. $3 \times 400 = 1200$
   $30 \times 400 = 12,000$

8 $60 \times 300 =$

9 $20 \times 800 =$

10 $40 \times 400 =$

11 $500 \times 30 =$

12 $70 \times 200 =$

13 $400 \times 30 =$

Explore

Try this multiplication trick.

Give a friend a 1p and a 20p coin to hold, one in each hand – hidden from you!

Tell them to work out 6 lots of the coin in their left hand, and 7 lots of the coin in their right hand.

Work out the total. If it is even the 1p is in their left hand, if it is odd the 1p is in their right hand.

Why does this work?

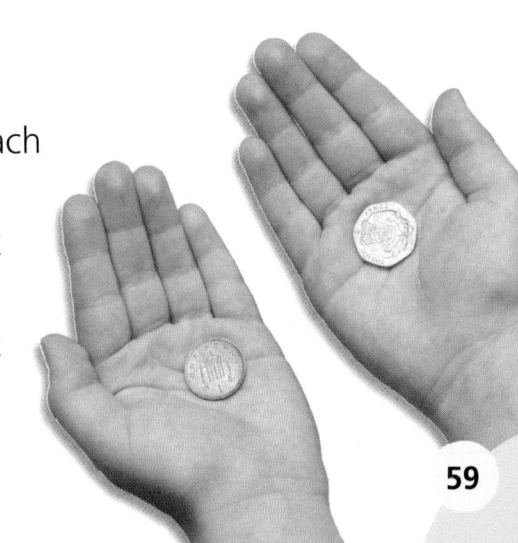

Multiplying

 **54 seats**    **62 seats**    **46 seats**    **24 seats**    **38 seats**

> Write how many seats.

1

1. $3 \times 54 = (3 \times 50) + (3 \times 4)$
   $= 150 + 12$
   $= 162$

2

3

4

5

6

7

8

9

10

🖋 Write how many seats for 8 of each vehicle.

> Copy and complete.

11  3×27

12 4×35

11. $3 \times 27 = (3 \times 20) + (3 \times 7)$
    $= 60 + 21$
    $= 81$

13 6×27 **14** 8×35 **15** 5×74 **16** 9×31

17 7×28 **18** 36×4 **19** 27×5 **20** 32×3

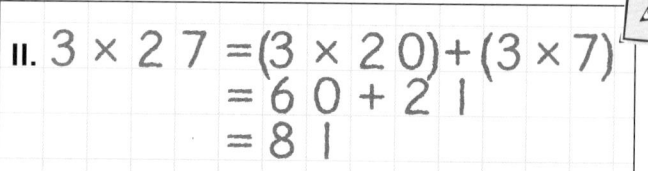

Multiplying

Write how many sweets in total.

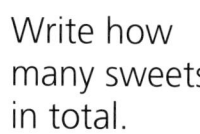

1. $6 \times 34 = (6 \times 30) + (6 \times 4)$
$= 180 + 24$
$= 204$

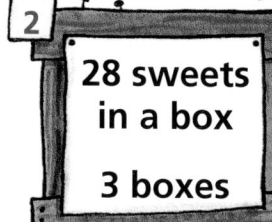

2. 28 sweets in a box

3 boxes

3. 55 sweets in a box

5 boxes

4. 46 sweets in a box

6 boxes

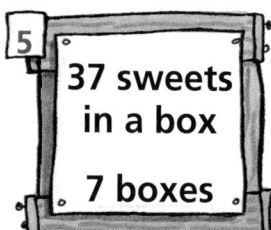

5. 37 sweets in a box

7 boxes

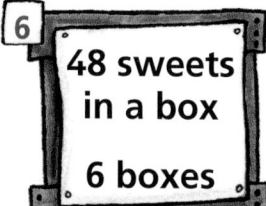

6. 48 sweets in a box

6 boxes

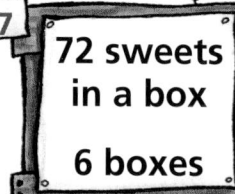

7. 72 sweets in a box

6 boxes

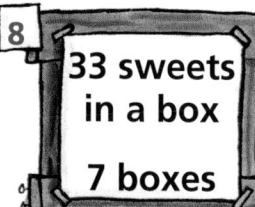

8. 33 sweets in a box

7 boxes

9. 42 sweets in a box

8 boxes

10. 37 sweets in a box

3 boxes

11. 54 sweets in a box

8 boxes

12. 62 sweets in a box

7 boxes

13. 35 sweets in a box

7 boxes

e Write how many sweets for 9 boxes of each.

Explore

Use the number cards and sign cards shown.

Use them to make a multiplication:

6 × 3 7 =

What is the smallest answer you can make? What is the largest?

How many other answers are there?

$6 \times 37 = 180 + 42$

£2·70   £3·20   £4·60   £5·30

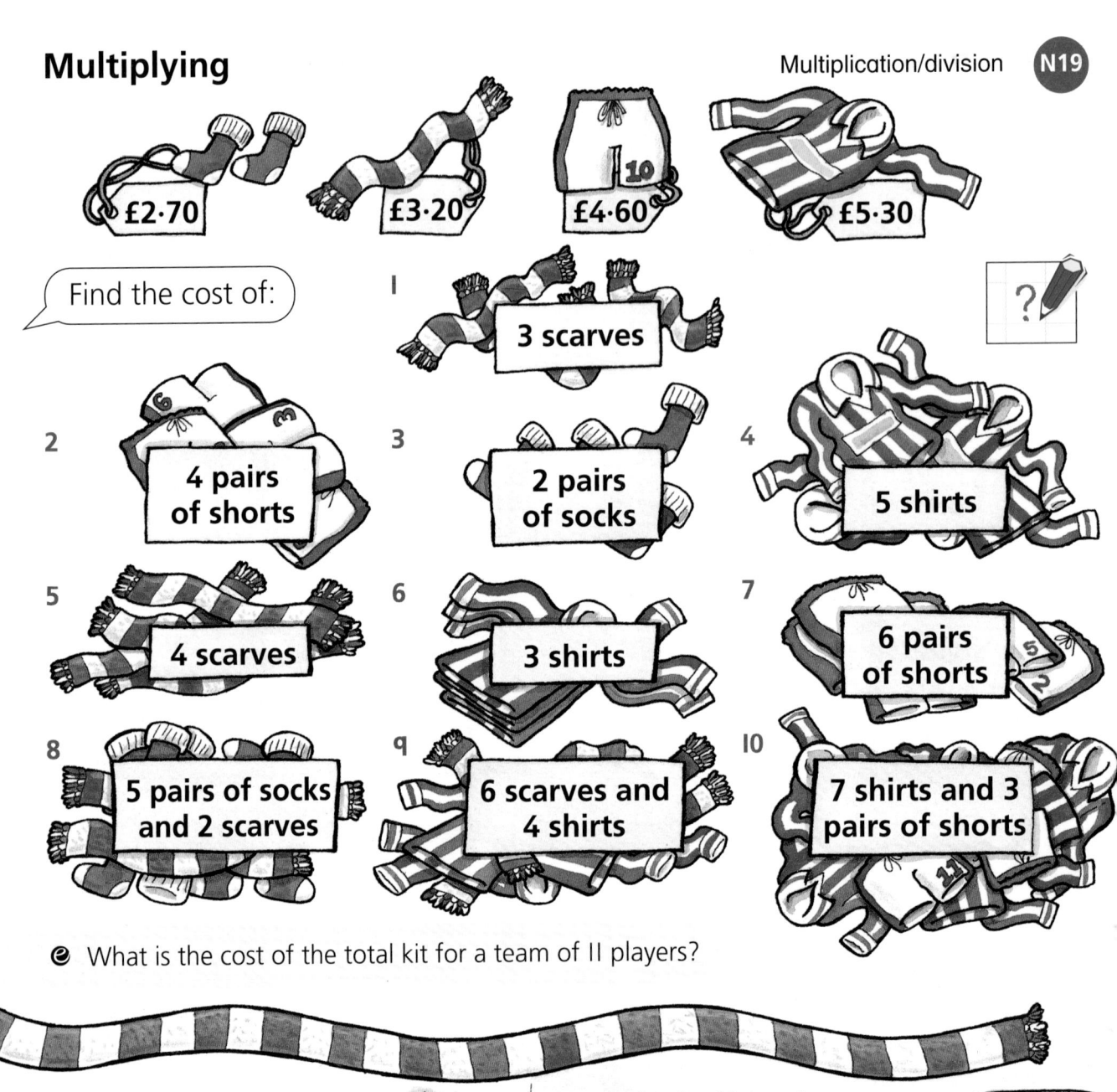

Find the cost of:

1 3 scarves

?

2 4 pairs of shorts

3 2 pairs of socks

4 5 shirts

5 4 scarves

6 3 shirts

7 6 pairs of shorts

8 5 pairs of socks and 2 scarves

9 6 scarves and 4 shirts

10 7 shirts and 3 pairs of shorts

ℯ What is the cost of the total kit for a team of 11 players?

Problems

11 Kiyoko's birthday is **23** weeks away.

How many days until her birthday?

12 A loaf of bread has **20** slices.

Will eats **5** slices of bread every day for **4** weeks.

How many loaves has he eaten?

13 An aeroplane has **7** seats in each row.

There are **56** rows of seats.

How many passengers can fly on the plane?

14 The Ghost Train has **22** carriages.

Each carriage has room for **4** people.

If **120** people are in the queue, how many must wait for the next train?

Dividing by 4

Write a quarter of each amount.

I.
$£52 ÷ 2 = £26$
$£26 ÷ 2 = £13$
$\frac{1}{4}$ of $£52 = £13$

1  £52

2  £72

3  £120

4  £66

5  £96

6  £60

7  £84

8  £132

9  £156

e Write how much 4 of each item cost.

Each garden is square.

Write the length of a side.

10

perimeter 24 m

10.
$24 m ÷ 2 = 12 m$
$12 m ÷ 2 = 6 m$

11

perimeter 56 m

12

perimeter 28 m

13

perimeter 92 m

14

perimeter 116 m

15

perimeter 148 m

16

perimeter 136 m

Dividing by 8

Teams are 8-a-side. | Write how many teams can be made.

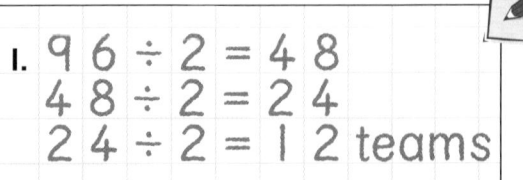

1. $96 \div 2 = 48$
$48 \div 2 = 24$
$24 \div 2 = 12$ teams

1
96 players

2
72 players

3
128 players

4
168 players

5
136 players

6
104 players

7
152 players

8
216 players

9
272 players

Copy and complete.

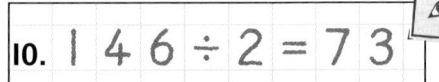

10. $146 \div 2 = 73$

10   $146 \div 2 = $

11   $104 \div 8 = $

12   $64 \div 4 = $

13   $238 \div 2 = $

14   $128 \div 8 = $

15   $76 \div 4 = $

16   $140 \div 8 = $

17   $424 \div 4 = $

18   $486 \div 2 = $

Dividing by halving first

Each group has won some money.

Write how much each person gets.

I. $£132 ÷ 2 = £66$
$£66 ÷ 3 = £22$

1. £132 — 6 people

2. £54 — 6 people

Start by halving.

3. £96 — 6 people

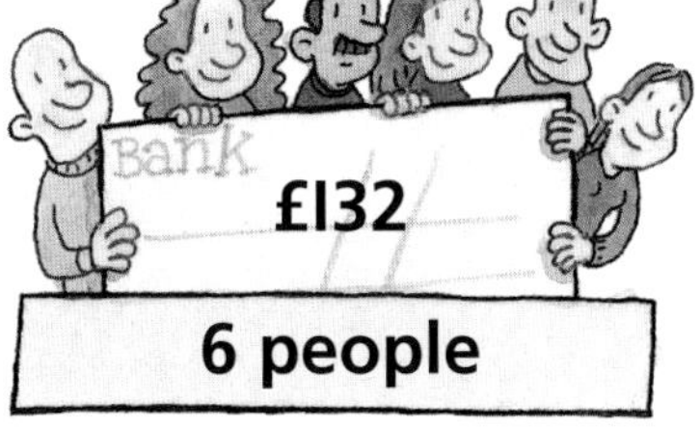

4. £84 — 12 people

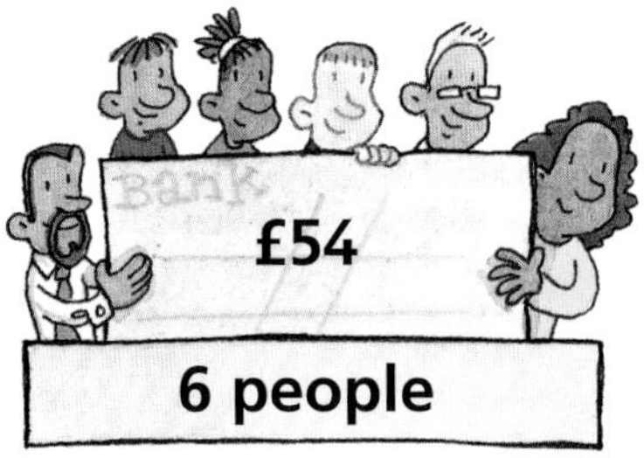

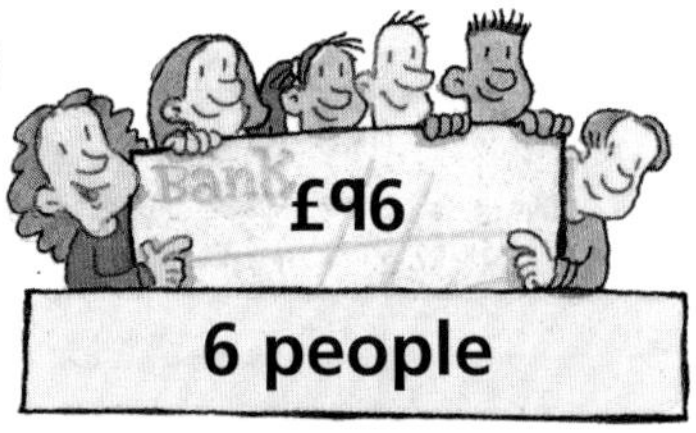

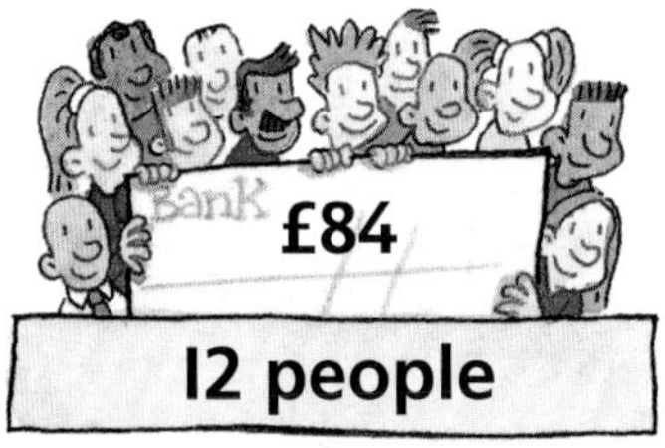

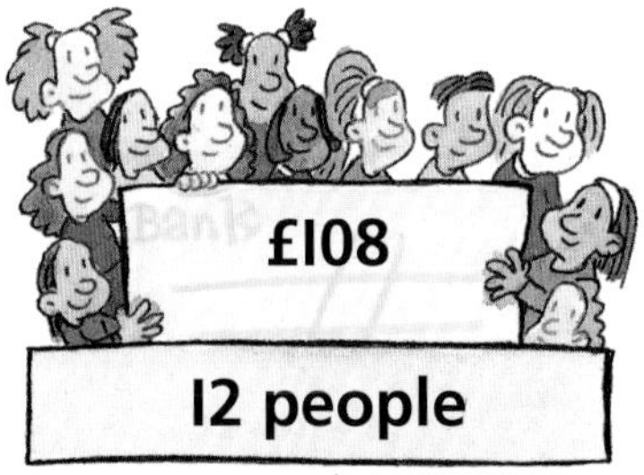

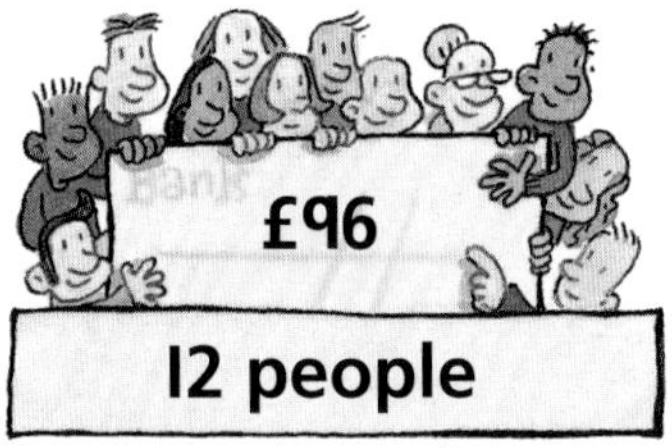

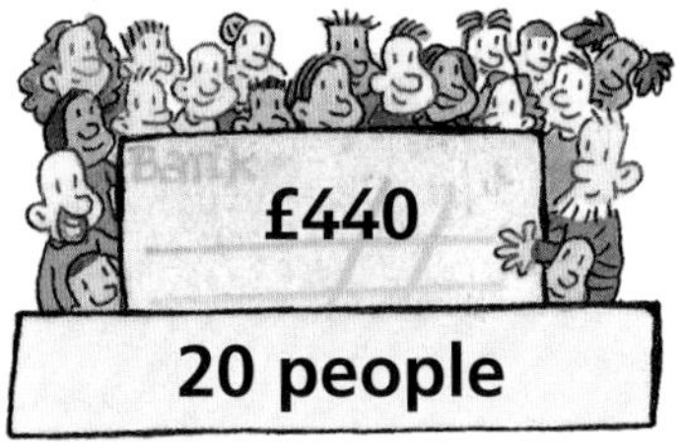

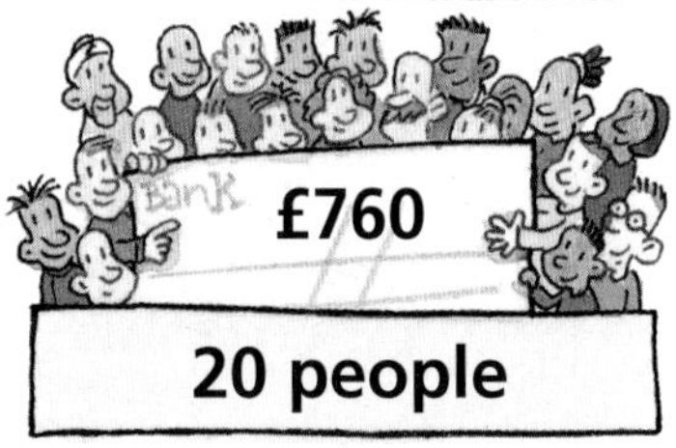

5. £108 — 12 people

6. £96 — 12 people

7. £440 — 20 people

8. £760 — 20 people

9. £840 — 20 people

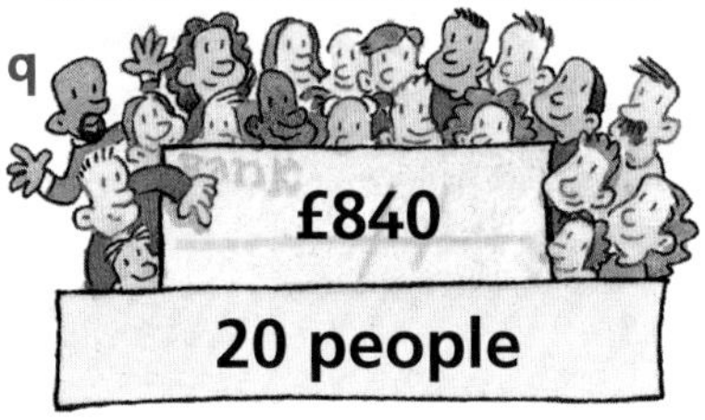

10. £1280 — 40 people

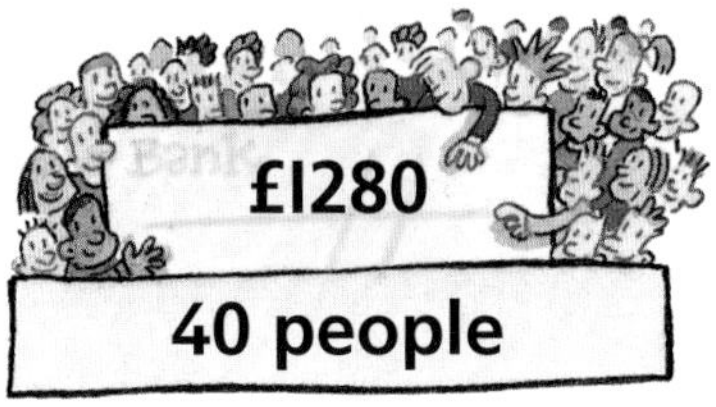

11. £4640 — 40 people

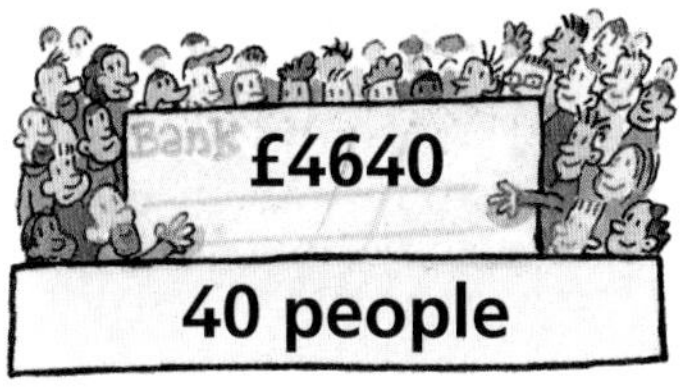

℮ How much does each person get if the size of each group doubles?

Explore

96 can be divided exactly by 16.

You can divide by 16 by halving, halving again, halving again and halving again.

Check that 96 can be divided exactly by 16.

Which of these numbers can be divided exactly by 16?

Find some numbers which divide exactly by 32.

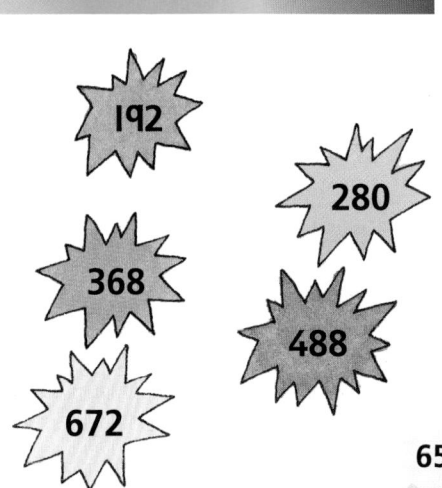

192

280

368

488

672

Write the position of each cone.

1. a = 2·2 4 m

1

a　b　c　d

2·2 m　2·3 m　2·4 m

2

a　b　c　d

3·6 m　3·7 m　3·8 m

3

a　b　c　d

4·1 m　4·2 m　4·3 m

e Write each position in centimetres.

Write the letter which matches each number.

4. C

A　B　C　D　E　F

2·5　2·6　2·7　2·8

G　H　I　J

4 ⟨2·63⟩　5 ⟨2·77⟩　6 ⟨2·61⟩　7 ⟨2·54⟩　8 ⟨2·55⟩

9 ⟨2·68⟩　10 ⟨2·66⟩　11 ⟨2·59⟩　12 ⟨2·73⟩　13 ⟨2·75⟩

Ordering decimals

Write < or > for each pair.

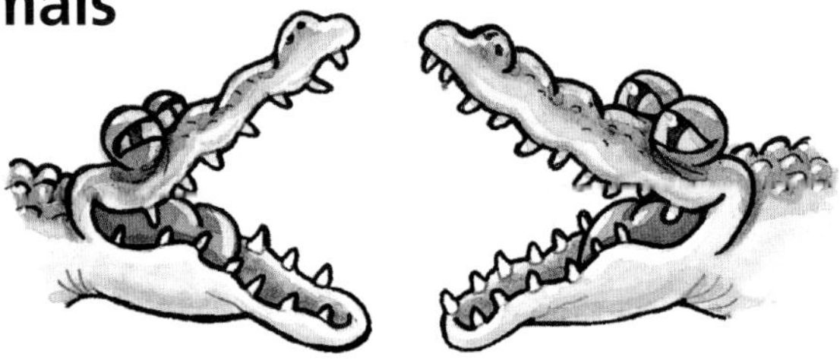

1. $1 \cdot 3 \, 4 < 1 \cdot 4 \, 3$

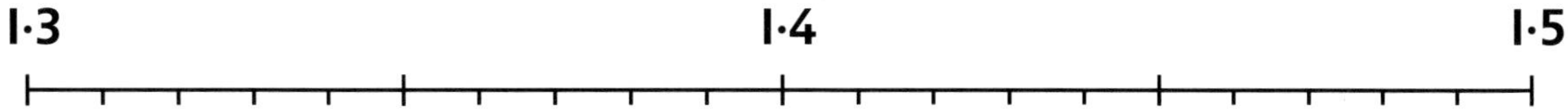

1·3   1·4   1·5

1 1·34, 1·43
2 1·4, 1·39
3 1·49, 1·39
4 1·31, 1·33
5 1·5, 1·49
6 1·72, 1·78
7 3·09, 3·12
8 3·48, 3·84
9 7·7, 7·8
10 10·01, 10·09
11 9·19, 9·2
12 9·07, 9·7

e Write all the decimals in order, ignoring repeats.

Write each weight.

13 3·3 — kg — 3·4

13. $3 \cdot 3 \, 3 \, k \, g$

14 6·6 — kg — 6·7

15 8·1 — kg — 8·2

16 10·0 — kg — 10·1

17 0 — kg — 0·1

18 0·1 — kg — 0·2

19 0·9 — kg — 1·0

Write the weights in order.

$0 \cdot 0 \, 7 \, kg, \, 0 \cdot 1 \, 3 \, kg \, ...$

67

Write the times in order, from fastest to slowest.

Name	Time (seconds)
Jon	56·7
Ashley	56·68
Sam	56·79
Dev	56·66
Amar	56·71
Zoe	56·69
Anu	56·61
Tara	56·8
Emile	56·59
Katy	56·62

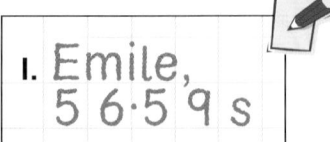

I. Emile, 56·59 s

Write the times in order, from fastest to slowest.

Name	Time (seconds)
A	10·1
B	10·58
C	10·01
D	10·98
E	10·23
F	10·4
G	10·04
H	10·67

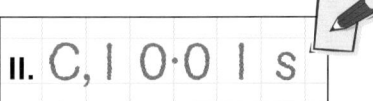

II. C, 10·01 s

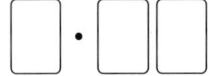

Explore

Use number cards 3, 7, 5 and 0.

Choose 3 cards to make decimal numbers of the form: ☐·☐☐

How many different numbers can you make? How many are less than 5? How many are more than 5? Write all the numbers in order, from smallest to largest.

Decimals and fractions

> Each animal grows by 1 cm.

> Write the new heights.

1. 3·69 m + 0·01 m = 3·70 m

1  3·69 m

2  2·76 m

3  5·16 m

4  1·17 m

5  1·62 m

6  2·29 m

7  1·21 m

8  0·26 m

9  1·84 m

ℯ Each animal grows by another 10 cm. Write the new heights.

> Write each fraction as a decimal.

10 $1\frac{7}{10}$

10. $1\frac{7}{10} = 1·7$

11 $2\frac{3}{10}$

12 $2\frac{5}{10}$

13  $\frac{6}{10}$

14 $1\frac{34}{100}$

15  $3\frac{36}{100}$

16  $2\frac{71}{100}$

17 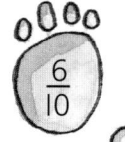 $14\frac{1}{10}$

18  $1\frac{60}{100}$

19  $23\frac{2}{10}$

20  $\frac{38}{100}$

21  $6\frac{8}{10}$

22  $1\frac{2}{100}$

23  $3\frac{1}{100}$

24  $1\frac{5}{10}$

25  $2\frac{1}{2}$

26 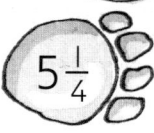 $5\frac{1}{4}$

Decimals and fractions

Write the new decimal numbers.

1 **1·75**

1. $1·75 + 0·1 = 1·85$
$1·85 - 0·01 = 1·84$
$1·84 + 0·1 = 1·94$
$1·94 - 0·01 = 1·93$

add $\frac{1}{10}$ subtract $\frac{1}{100}$ add $\frac{1}{10}$ subtract $\frac{1}{100}$

2 **4·81**   3 **9·98**   4 **7·02**   5 **6·80**

6 **5·10**   7 **3·00**   8 **2·61**   9 **8·39**

10 **6·48**   11 **7·50**   12 **1·34**   13 **10·23**

e Subtract $\frac{3}{10}$ and then add $\frac{5}{100}$ to each number.

Write each decimal as a mixed number.

14 **2·7**

14. $2·7 = 2\frac{7}{10}$

15 **1·9**   16 **5·5**   17 **1·22**   18 **10·1**   19 **3·76**

20 **0·7**   21 **9·09**   22 **13·3**   23 **4·04**   24 **15·6**

25 **0·81**   26 **5·7**   27 **0·06**   28 **0·5**   29 **1·25**

Decimals and fractions

Write the length of each snake in metres.

1

1 m 28 cm

1. 1·28 m

2

4 m 99 cm

3

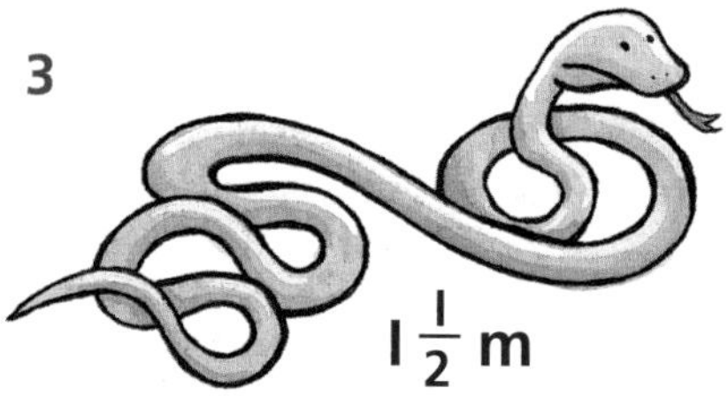

$1\frac{1}{2}$ m

4

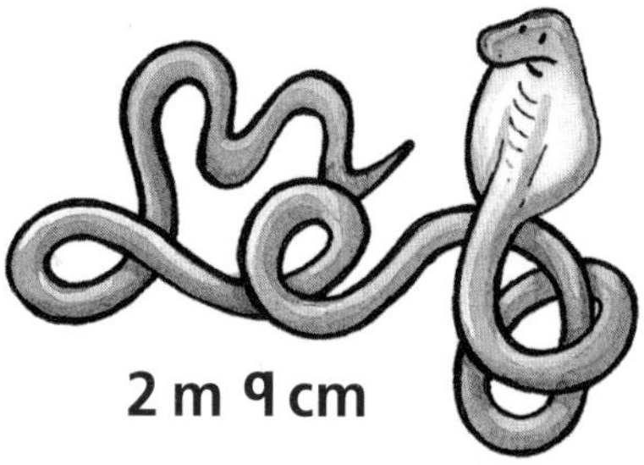

2 m 9 cm

5

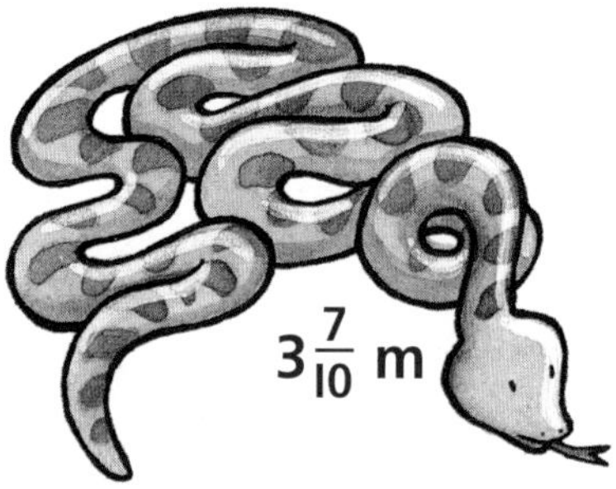

$3\frac{7}{10}$ m

6

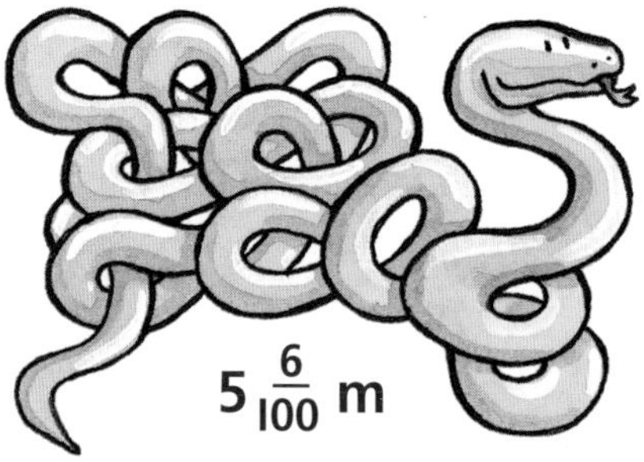

$5\frac{6}{100}$ m

7

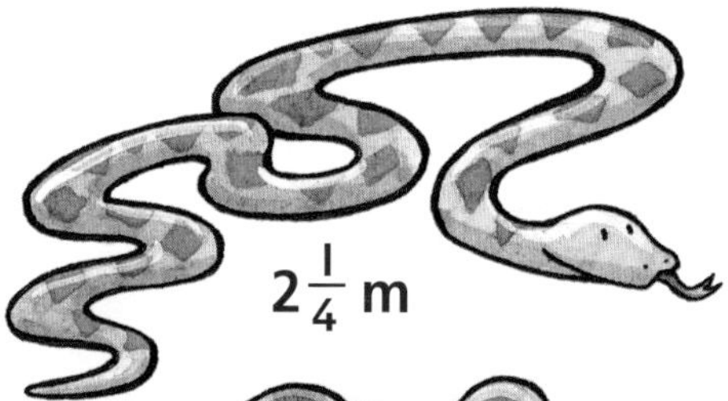

$2\frac{1}{4}$ m

8 2 m 30 cm

9

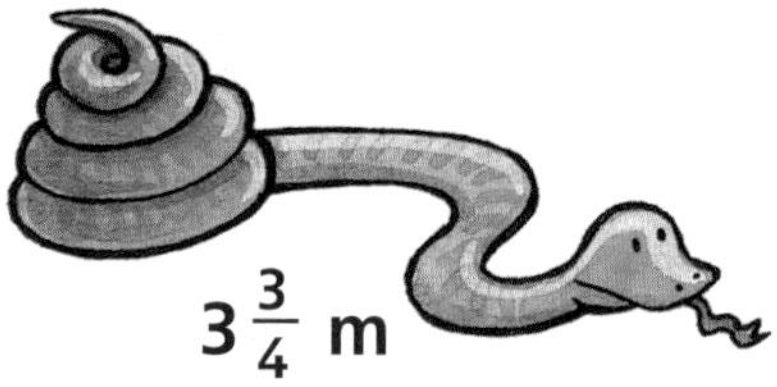

$3\frac{3}{4}$ m

10

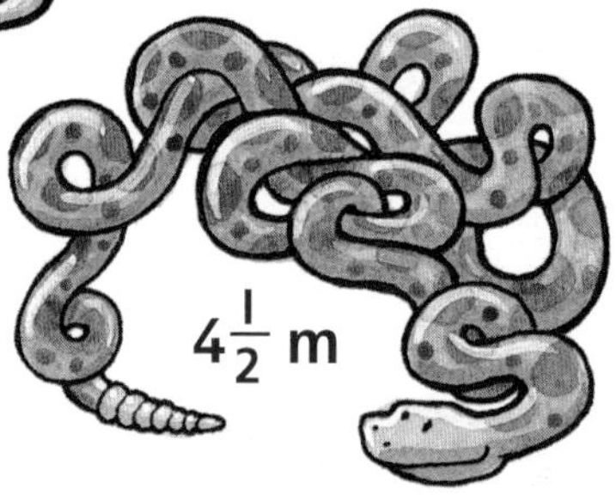

$4\frac{1}{2}$ m

ℯ Each snake grows 25 cm. Write the new lengths.

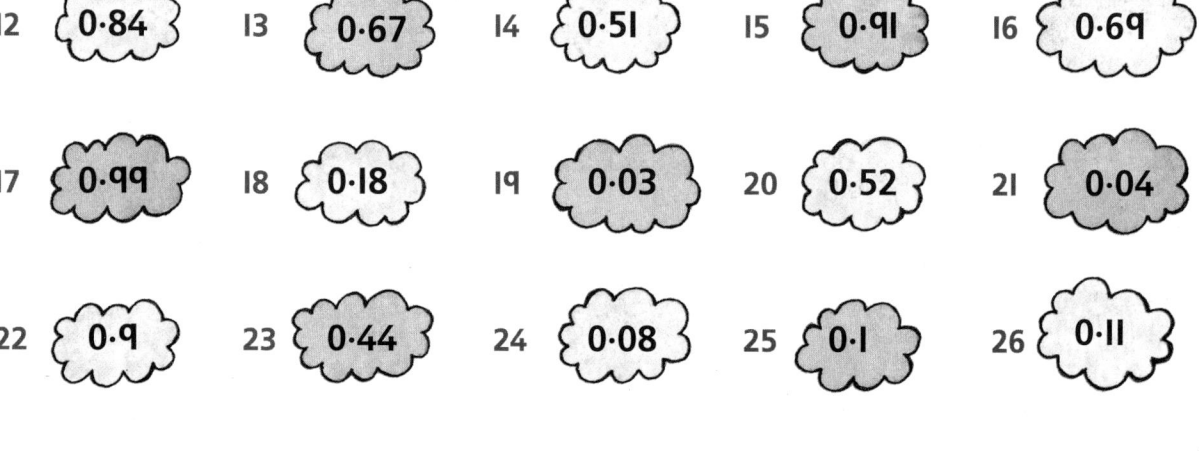

Write how many tenths and hundredths.

11 0·71

11. $0·71 = \frac{7}{10} + \frac{1}{100}$

12 0·84   13 0·67   14 0·51   15 0·91   16 0·69

17 0·99   18 0·18   19 0·03   20 0·52   21 0·04

22 0·9   23 0·44   24 0·08   25 0·1   26 0·11

Mixed problems

1 Sean scores **1040** points on his computer game.

He loses a life and his score goes down by **100** points.

He collects more treasure and adds **206** points to his score.

He takes the wrong turn and his score is divided by **10**.

How many points does he have now?

---

2 Naima is organising a birthday party for her friend.

She needs to buy drinks, burgers and fries for **14** people.

The birthday cake costs **£7·50**.

Drinks cost **42p** each.
Burgers cost **£1·49** each.
Fries cost **59p** each.

She has **£50** to spend.

How much money does she have left to buy a present?

---

3 George is making a tape for his dad.

There are **3** songs which are $4\frac{1}{2}$ minutes long, **4** songs which are $2\frac{1}{4}$ minutes, **2** songs which are $5\frac{1}{2}$ minutes and **1** song that is **6** minutes long.

Will all the songs fit on the tape?

The tape is **40** minutes long.

By how many minutes is the tape too long or too short?

---

4 Caitlin is on a cycling holiday.

The next day she rides **39 km**.

Then she has to cycle home again.

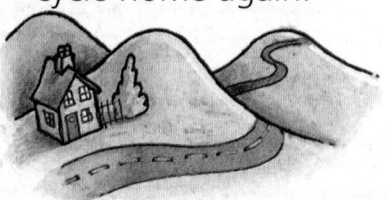

On the first day she rides **25 km**.

The day after she rides to the sea. It is double the distance she rode on the second day.

How far does she travel in total?